excel 2000
made
painless

A CIP Catalogue for this book is available from the British Library

ISBN 1 85868 934 1

Project Editor: Lara Maiklem
Production: Sarah Corteel

Created by Gecko Grafx Ltd

Notice of Liability
Every effort has been made to ensure that this book contains accurate and current information. However, the Publisher and the author shall not be liable for any loss or damage suffered by the readers as a result of any information contained herein.

Trademarks
Microsoft® Excel 2000®, Office 2000® and Windows® are registered trademarks of Microsoft Corporation.
All other trademarks are acknowledged as belonging to their respective companies

Printed and bound in Italy

excel 2000 made painless

Christophe Dillinger

CARLTON BOOKS

CONTENTS

GETTING STARTED

1

To start off, we're going to look into the very basics of starting with Excel 2000. First, we'll explain how to install it on your computer and start it up. We'll then discuss some of the initial preparation that you should consider in order to make use easier later on, and tell you about the things that you really ought to keep in mind at all times when using the program.

INSTALLING EXCEL

First of all, we're going to look at how to set up Microsoft's Excel 2000 to run on your computer, and what you might want to use it for. It is always worth taking a few moments to get things right when you install new software, because the the minutes you take right now could save you hours or even days in the future if you have any problems.

WHAT DO YOU NEED?

Microsoft Excel 2000 comes as part of the Microsoft Office suite of programs, which also includes the Word 2000 word processor, PowerPoint 2000 presentation program and Outlook 2000 email program. There are several different versions of the Microsoft Office 2000, and they have slightly different system requirements.

The standard requirements are shown in the box below. If you're not sure about what it means, don't worry. The requirements are quite modest, and most computers purchased in the last two or three years should be able to run Excel 2000 without problems.

WHAT DO YOU NEED?

The Standard version of Office requires a Pentium 75mhz computer or better, and Windows 95 or later. It can also run on an NT Workstation running version 3, System Pack 4 or later. You'll need to have at least 16 MB of Ram (32 for NT) and 189 MB of free disk space on your hard drive. You'll also need a CD-Rom drive, and a VGA or better monitor.

INSTALLING EXCEL 2000

If you already have Excel loaded on your computer, you can skip forward to the next section. Otherwise, follow the simple instructions below.

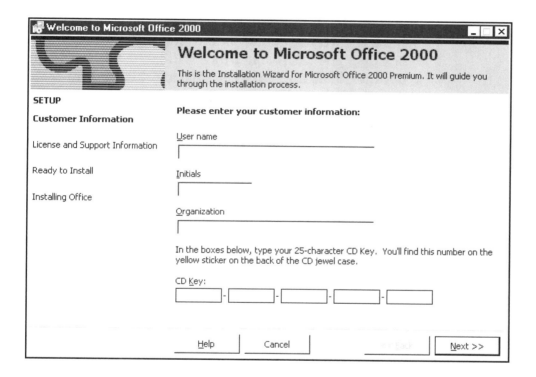

Close any program you currently have running, then insert the Microsoft Office CD Rom into the CD Drive. It will automatically start the Install program. When prompted, enter your name and company (if any), and the security key code from the CD case. Make absolutely certain that you get your unique, personal CD Key correct, because without it you will not be able to install Excel or, later, get any assistance from Microsoft. If you do mis-type it, don't worry, you'll get plenty of chances to get it right!

STANDARD INSTALLATION

Unless you specifically want to make some alterations to Microsoft's recommended installation, tell the install program to proceed with a standard set-up by clicking on Install Now. This will install Excel, along with the tools it needs to function properly, and the other Microsoft Office programs included with Excel, such as Microsoft Word. You will be shown the details, and asked if you want to proceed. Click OK. The Microsoft Office will be installed on your computer. This may take several minutes, and the install program will need to restart your computer before it can finish off. Once it has done everything and returned you to Windows, you are ready to run Excel.

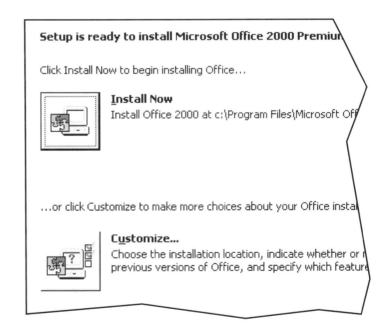

Setup is ready to install Microsoft Office 2000 Premium

Click Install Now to begin installing Office...

Install Now
Install Office 2000 at c:\Program Files\Microsoft Off

...or click Customize to make more choices about your Office insta

Customize...
Choose the installation location, indicate whether or
previous versions of Office, and specify which feature

CUSTOM INSTALLATIONS

If you want to use Excel without installing the rest of the Microsoft Office software – if you were very short on hard disk space, for example, or simply had no use for a word processor – then it is possible to install Excel on its own. To do this, you select Customize during installation.

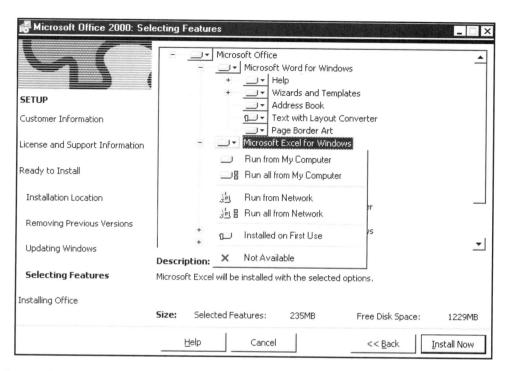

Click on a box and select <u>Run all from My Computer</u> if you want to make sure that specific program installs fully.

The installation program will show you a list of possible components that are available with your version of Office 2000. Next to each component is a little box which shows what is being installed for that category – a white box with a disk in it means all of that program and its subcomponents will be installed; the same image with a "1"overlaid means that all of the program will be shown as available, but fully installed when it is first used; a grey box with a disk means that some parts of it will be installed; and a red cross means that none of it will be installed. A "+" sign to the left of the box means that there are subcomponents available to select. Click on the + to expand the list of subcomponents – you can choose specific tools and elements that go with each part of the Office to install, install later or not install at all. You're only shown optional extras, so Excel would run with none of its sub-components installed, but as you will lose a lot of extra functionality that way, it is not advised unless you need the disk space. When you are happy with the Office programs and components to be installed, click <u>Install Now</u>.

Managing Excel Documents

Having a well thought-out set of folders for your documents will make your life a lot easier once you've been using Excel for a while. If you put everything in the same folder without thinking too much about what you're calling your documents, the time will come when you're faced with a long list of obscurely-titled files, and it will be difficult and time-consuming to work out which one you want. Preparing a good structure for your folders will repay you well in the long run.

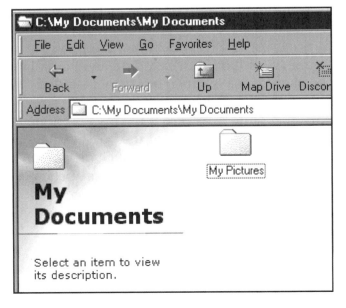

WHERE TO STORE DOCUMENTS

The best place to start your own personal set of document folders is inside the folder titled My Documents, which you will find is already on your desktop. Excel, like other programs in the Microsoft Office, is already set to work with this folder, so it makes the best choice for a starting point. If you've been using programs from the Microsoft Office before, you may well find that there are already Office documents inside My Documents. That isn't going to be a problem.

CREATING YOUR OWN FOLDERS
Setting up your own folders inside My Documents is easy.

1 Double-click on the My Documents icon on your desktop, and it will open up. Then place the mouse pointer inside the open folder, and right-click. A menu of tools will open up next to your pointer. Hold the pointer over the selection New, and a new documents sub-menu will appear. The top option is Folder; click on that.

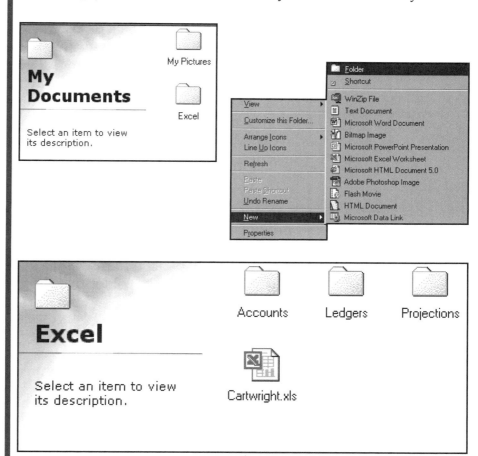

2 A new folder will appear next to the mouse pointer, called New Folder. Anything you type now, before you press the mouse again, will become the folder's new name. We suggest you call this folder Excel.

3 Double-click on the new Excel folder, and it too will open. You can now follow the process in 1 and 2 above to create a new folder for each different category of document you will be creating with Microsoft Excel 2000. This can be folders named after clients for accounts, or by different types of function – graphs, spreadsheets, lists and so on – or even just as simple a division as calling folders Personal and Business. You can also add further folders inside any folder you create here – so Business could have subfolders Incoming and Outgoing, and you can store Excel documents inside this folder too, if they don't fit any of the categories you've created.

OPENING DOCUMENTS

There are two ways to open an Excel document. If you are in
Windows but Excel is not running, the quickest way to open a
document is to double-click on it. This will start Microsoft Excel
up automatically, load your document into Excel, and present it
ready for you to start working on. All you have to do is find
where the document is stored – within the sub-folder Excel
inside the desktop folder My Documents, if you have set up a
file structure as we recommend – and double-click its icon.

If you have Excel already running, you can open a file by
selecting the Open command from the File menu. This will
give you the Open dialog box, which shows you the
contents of your My Documents folder by default. You can
then double-click on the Excel folder within the box to enter it,
continue through your folder structure to the file you want,
and then double-click on it to load it into Excel. You can also
use the "Back Up" icon to move one step backwards inside
your folders, to see the folder that holds the one you are
currently looking at.

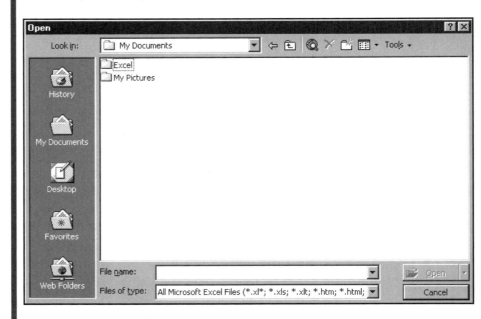

Opening an Excel file: this is the window you'll see after clicking on Open in
the File menu with Excel already running.

SAVING DOCUMENTS

To save an existing workbook, simply select <u>Save</u> from the <u>File</u> menu. If the workbook is one you have just created, you will need to give it a name, and tell the computer where to store it. Select <u>Save As</u> from the <u>File</u> menu, and you will get a dialog box called <u>Save As</u>, which is similar to the <u>Open</u> dialog. Navigate through to the folder you want to save it in by double-clicking your way through your structure as before, then type the name you want the document to be called in the box <u>File Name</u>, and click <u>Save</u>. Try to make sure that the document name explains the contents – "2000MarchAccounts" for example. If you use obscure file names, like "KDFRpt1", in time you may forget what the file was for.

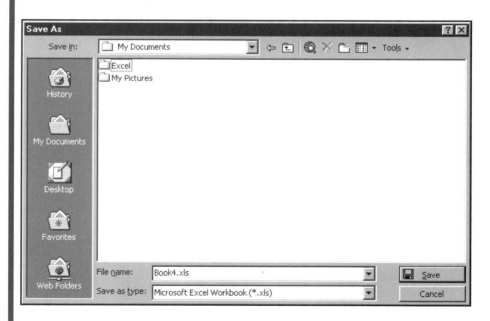

Saving an Excel file: this is the window you'll see after clicking on <u>Save as</u> in the <u>File</u> menu. Choose a name and a destination for your file and click <u>Save</u>.

You can also save your documents as other types of file, for different programs to read. More details will be provided later, but this is achieved by clicking on the selection "down arrow" tab at the right hand side of the <u>Save as type</u> box below the file name.

PASSWORD PROTECTION

It is possible to restrict access to your Excel files, for greater safety. If you click on the <u>Tools</u> selection tab in the top right of the <u>Save As</u> dialog box, you'll get a list of options for your saved file. Click on the <u>General</u> line, and a <u>Save Options</u> box will appear. Type a password inside either of the boxes indicated under the <u>File Sharing</u> title, then click <u>OK</u>. When the document is loaded, Excel will ask for a password. Typing in the <u>Password to Open</u> password (with the same capitalization) will let the person look at the document but not change it or save it; typing in the other password will let them use the file as normal.

When you are choosing a password for your files, it is always sensible to use something that could not be found in a dictionary. It is best to include at least one capital letter and at least one number, so as to increase the difficulty of someone else guessing it. For example, "OranGes8" is a much better password than just "oranges" or even "Oranges8". Make sure you can remember your passwords though, or else you will be locked out of your own files.

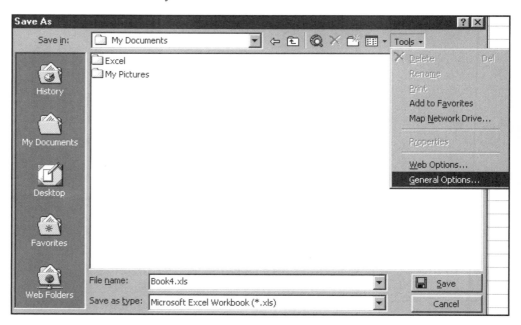

Using the <u>Tools</u> menu in the <u>Save As</u> dialog box. You can set and change passwords by selecting <u>General Options</u> and then <u>File Sharing</u>.

CREATING BACKUPS

The other important possibility provided by the <u>Save Options</u> box on the previous page is the one labeled <u>Always create backup</u>. This makes sure that whenever you save a document, the old version that you are replacing is stored, under the name of "Backup Of ABC.xlk", where ABC is the name of your file. This can be a real help when it comes to recovering from a mistake. It is all too easy to make a mistake with your document – such as deleting some vital data – and then save it before you notice. With a backup, so long as you have only saved the mistake once, a correct version of your document will still be available to you. This can be invaluable.

HARD BACKUPS

A more permanent and secure option is to create physical backups of your files on a regular basis. It is well worth copying files that you work on regularly to floppy disks (or Zip/Jaz disks, Syquest cartridges, or other removable storage devices) and storing them in a different location to the computer. The more important a document is and the more frequently you work on it, the more often you should create a hard backup like this. If you can afford enough disks, it is best to keep old versions of the document (clearly labelled as such) so that if there is a problem that has been ongoing for some time, you can get a copy of the document from before the error arose.

Good backup procedure is particularly vital with Microsoft Excel because it is often used to store key data. Keep a backup disk for each day of the week, and save your data every night to that day's disk, over-writing the last week's information. For Fridays, keep five disks, one for each week of the month, and always save over the oldest data, so that at any one time you have daily backups for the last week, and weekly backups for the last month. On the last week of the month, do not use the old disk, but put it in a secure store and use a new disk. That way, you'll have an archive of monthly backups available if something goes wrong – a company-saving resource if your accounting computer crashes or is stolen.

STARTING A NEW DOCUMENT

Excel makes it simple to start working right away with a clean sheet. When you start the program by clicking on its icon, you are presented with a new workbook that you may immediately make use of, and if, at any time, you want a new fresh workbook to utilize, you can click on the <u>New Workbook</u> icon just underneath the <u>File</u> menu. However, starting from scratch is just one of your options.

The New Workbook icon.

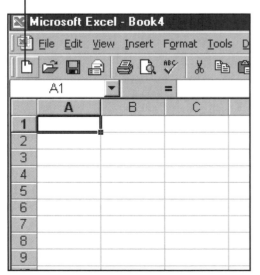

STARTING FROM A TEMPLATE

A template is a type of Excel file that can act as the starting point for many different workbooks. Depending on the amount of information stored in the template – which can include formatting commands, data, macros and even entire charts – the effect can be as simple as providing you with a consistent look and feel for your worksheets or as complex as offering you powerful pre-built forms.

Excel comes with several complex templates provided. These are easily customized to your personal situation, and include an expenses form, a standard invoice, and a standard purchase order. There is also an order form for purchasing further pre-made templates from a particular third party company. Each template is easy to personalise. Once you have entered your own data, saving the document creates a new template based on your personal information.

OPENING A TEMPLATE

To work with any template, whether one of Excel's provided ones or one of your own, you need to start a new document from the <u>File</u> menu.

1 Select <u>New</u> from the <u>File</u> menu

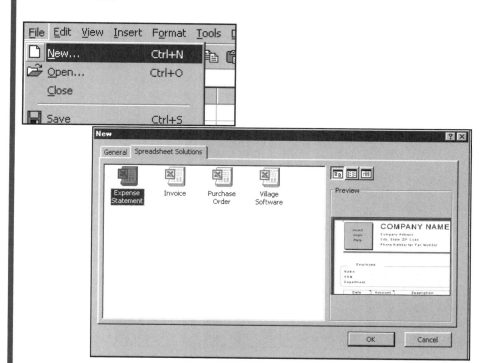

2 The <u>New</u> dialog box comes up. In the <u>General</u> tab, which is the one you see first, will be the blank workbook file you usually start with, called Workbook, and any templates you have saved yourself. Click on the other tabs to access the template forms that are provided with Excel.

CREATING A NEW TEMPLATE

The templates that Excel provides will automatically save in the correct place once customized. However, you can easily save a file of your own as a new template. Your new template can be as extensive or as simple as you like, from simply having headings filled in at the top of columns to your own pre-created forms. To save a template, choose <u>Save As...</u> from the <u>File</u> menu, then type in the name as usual and click on the <u>Save As Type...</u> bar at the bottom of the dialog box. A list of possible types will drop down; select <u>Template (*.xlt)</u>, the third option from the top. Click <u>OK</u>, and the document will automatically be saved in with the other templates. From then on, the new template will appear in the <u>General</u> tab of the <u>New</u> dialog box.

THE GOLDEN RULES

There are three major things that you should do your best to keep in mind at all times when working with Excel. They are simple, but they will go a long way to making sure that everything goes smoothly. Without them, you will find yourself becoming vulnerable to lost data and extreme frustration. Few things are as depressing as spending hours working on a document only to lose all your hard work through a simple slip.

RULE NUMBER ONE:
BE CAREFUL WHEN OVER-WRITING A CELL

1 Always be aware of what you are over-writing in a cell.

C6	▼	=	Selected
	A	B	C	D	E	F
1						
2						
3						
4						
5						
6			Selected			
7						

When you have selected a cell that contains information, it is possible to erase everything within the cell by typing over it. This is a very easy mistake to make, and, if you keep your head, it is very easy to rectify. Cells can be protected, which makes it impossible to alter what is inside them, and you may want to protect certain critical cells at one time or another, to make sure that a complicated form or spreadsheet cannot be damaged. Cells are selected by clicking on them once. If you double-click on a cell, it will become active, and information that you type into it will generally be added to whatever is there already, rather than replacing it, so, in general, it will be safer to select cells that you want to edit by double-clicking. If you do make a mistake, move on to rule 2.

RULE NUMBER TWO: DON'T PANIC, JUST UNDO

When you have made a mistake, the first place to look for help is the Undo function. You can access it by selecting Undo at the

2 Remember the Undo feature if you have any problems.

top of the Edit menu, by clicking on the Undo icon on the main toolbar, or by holding Ctrl down and pressing Z (Ctrl-Z).

Undo works by storing a record of everything you do to your document, in the order you do it in. Then, if you want to undo something you have done – even after a short period of time – you can select Undo, item by item, until the mistake has been corrected. If you over-write some information you needed (or even erase the data in your entire worksheet by accident, which is very difficult), just Undo the mistake and it will be as if you had never made the mistake in the first place. If you then change your mind and want to re-do it, then the Redo command is situated next to the Undo command on the toolbar and menu.

The most important thing to remember about Undo – apart from the fact that it is there for you – is that it only works on mistakes made since you last loaded the document. If you make a serious mistake, do not, under *any* circumstances, save the flawed document over the older, previously correct document. Don't close or save the wrong document until you've tried to correct things with <u>Undo</u>, and if you do save it, use a new name so that you at least have the earlier versions to fall back on.

RULE NUMBER THREE: SAVE OFTEN

The best way of protecting yourself against mistakes and computer crashes is to save the documents that you are working on regularly. Excel will automatically save recovery files for you in case the machine crashes, and it will automatically create a backup of the last version of the file for you, but neither of these protections are quite as safe as making sure that you save your file regularly. If you are busy with a lengthy project, it is worth pausing every 15 minutes to check that your work is correct and then, once you're happy

3 Don't forget to <u>Save</u> your work.

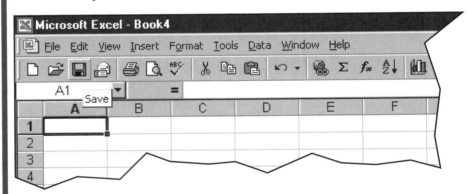

that it is right, saving the document. There is no substitute for saving your work. If you make a point of saving your document every fifteen minutes, then even in the most serious cases, the worst that can happen to you is that you lose the last 15 minutes of work.

In addition to selecting <u>Save</u> from the <u>File</u> menu, you can also access it in two slightly quicker ways. One is to click on the small disk icon near the left hand side of the main toolbar, and the other is to press <u>Control-S</u> on the keyboard. Both of those will perform a so-called Background Save, storing your data quickly without holding up the entire computer, so you can continue working.

ALL ABOUT CELLS

2

Cells are the basic building blocks of an Excel worksheet. They are arranged into a grid of rows – numbered from 1 onwards – and of columns, labelled from A to Z and then from AA to ZZ. Each cell holds one piece of information, which can range from a simple number or sentence to a complicated formula making use of special functions to analyse large sections of the rest of the workbook. In addition, cells can be joined together, modified in size and shape, tinted and filled, and worked in a number of ways to change their appearance.

ENTERING AND CHANGING DATA

The first thing you need in order to start using Excel efficiently is to understand how to use a cell to hold data. Entering data in a form that makes it easy to use later is at the heart of all Excel work. It's the most basic and important function. Fortunately, it's also easy to understand.

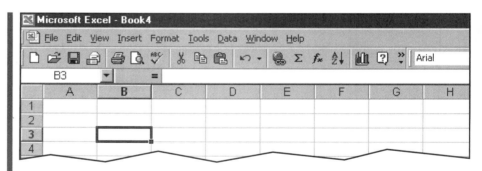

THE BASICS OF SELECTING A CELL

Left-clicking on a cell selects it and its contents. The cell is then ready for whatever operations you want to perform on it. A cell can be specified as one of a number of types, which means that it will only accept certain forms of information – numbers only, currency values, dates, raw text and others. A cell is referred to by its column and row in that order. In the diagram above, the selected cell – identified by its black border – is known as B3. The first cell in the worksheet is A1, but the theoretical last cell is very far away. You can keep adding as many rows as you need until your computer runs out of memory at row 65536, which would take a very long time.

ENTERING DATA

Once a blank cell is selected, you can simply type, and the information you provide will be stored in the cell. There are two types of data that a cell can hold, "constants", which are simply letters, numbers and certain other characters that do not change, and "formulas", which contain instructions to program Excel to perform certain tasks. Formulas will be discussed later in the book. Here, we're going to look at constants, particularly numerical data and text strings.

One cell can hold a lot of information. Although there may be too many characters to fit in the cell's apparent size on the screen, it can hold much more information than that. If we have a whole sentence in cell B3, then as long as the cells to the right of B3 – C3, D3, E3 and so on – are empty, the text in B3 will be shown as spilling over, although in truth it is all contained in B3. As soon as it reaches a cell with something in it, the remainder of the text will be hidden.

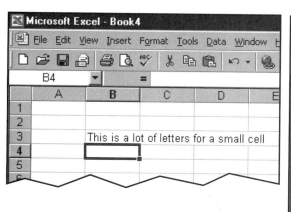 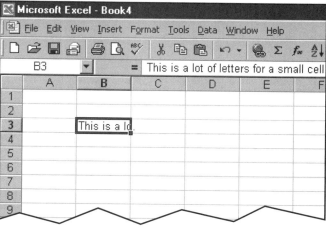

As you can see here, the image on the left shows the text in cell B3 spilling over to the right. The image on the right shows what you see when you type a period (.) in cell C3, so that it is no longer empty. The information in cell B3 does not change – just the part of it you can see on the sheet. If you select cell B3, you will see the entire contents of the cell in the cell contents box in the toolbar towards the top of the screen. Later, you will also learn how to make text wrap around to fit inside a cell, and to increase a cell's size.

CHANGING A CELL'S CONTENTS

Once information has been entered into a cell, it is easy to modify it. If you enter information into a cell, it stays active until you press <u>Return</u> (the cell below becomes the active one), <u>Tab</u> (the cell to the right becomes active), <u>Shift-Tab</u> (the cell to the left becomes active), or press a cursor key or click on a different cell. While it remains active, data can be deleted with the backspace key and retyped as normal. Once it is no longer active, the cell needs to be re-selected before the data inside it can be modified. The quickest way to do so is to select the cell as described on the prevous page, by left-clicking on it once. At this point, any new information you type will entirely replace the existing contents of the cell. While this is simple, it is also counter-productive if you merely want to edit the cell's contents rather than overwrite them.

If you want to edit the data rather than replace it, then once you have selected the cell you can click on the cell content box in the toolbar, as indicated left. You can use the mouse pointer to select the individual characters to replace or to position the cursor for editing, or use the backspace and delete keys. Alternatively, you can double-click on the cell you want to edit, which will bring the contents up in the cell itself for you to modify with the backspace and delete keys.

The cell contents box.

The cell in the image above has been clicked on once, to be edited. The cell to the right has been double-clicked on.

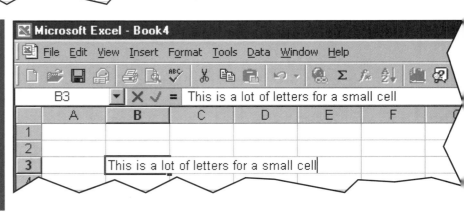

SPECIAL CHARACTERS

When you enter information into a cell, Excel tries to guess what type of data it is. It compares the contents of the cell to its list of different data types – we'll explain those in detail over the page – and if it isn't sure, it assumes the cell holds plain text. One of the easiest ways to tell whether Excel thinks a cell contains text or numbers is by the positioning – alignment – of the cell's contents. Plain text is normally stored starting at the left hand edge of the cell, and numbers are normally stored ending at the right hand edge, as shown below.

Cell B5 contains text, automatically left-aligned and C5 contains a number, automatically right-aligned.

Certain chararcters, if they are found in with numbers, change the way Excel thinks of the number – for example, parentheses around a number such as (200) are an accounting convention for debits, so Excel translates (200) to -200. Other characters that still count as numeric include currency symbols, %, and standard mathematical notation such as +445.1 or 68*4. Starting a cell with an = sign indicates you are entering a formula, which we'll deal with later. Excel will first try to convert a forward slash – / – to a date rather than a fraction, so if you want to enter a fraction that might be a date, such as 6/8, add a 0 and a space before the fraction, so it becomes 0 6/8 ("Zero and Six Eighths"). That way, Excel will understand.

Microsoft Excel - Book4

File Edit View Insert Format Tools Data Window

A1

	A	B	C	D
1				
2				
3				
4				
5		Text		23
6				
7				
8				
9				
10				
11				
12				
13				
14				
15				

MAKE IT TEXT

To make sure that Excel treats a cell as plain text, even if it is just a number, put an apostrophe symbol (a ') at the start of the data. Excel will then assign the cell to plain text.

DATA TYPES

Excel categorises the information you enter into a cell in a number of different ways. These are referred to as data types. Each different data type provides certain different options and abilities to you. Efficient use of data types will really help you make the most of working with Excel.

BASIC DATA TYPES

There are three basic types of data, which have already been discussed. **General** is the type given to a cell by default, and it becomes one of the other types according to Excel's needs when you enter some data. **Number** is the standard type for dealing with a numeric value. Decimals are displayed rounded to two places, although the full value is kept – i.e. 34,544.05. **Text** is used for storing non-numerical information, and presents the material exactly as you type it in – i.e. "Balloons". In addition, **Date** and **Time** are special data types used to present chronological information, and each has several different ways that they can be displayed – i.e. 13-Mar-00 and 13:50pm.

ACCOUNTS DATA TYPES

There are two main data types for accounts formats. **Currency** converts a number to a standard currency display, including removing leading 0s, adding the correct currency symbol, and a 2-digit decimal display – i.e. £4,450.00. **Accounting** format also converts a number to a currency display, but it lines up the column so that the currency symbols are lined up and the decimal places are lined up, like this:

```
£   45.50
£1233.00
£   69.99
```

MATHEMATICAL DATA TYPES

There are three special maths data types. **Percentage** displays the cell's contents as a percentile. If you type a number over 1 into a Percentage cell, it will be converted to a standard % with 2 decimal places. If you type in a decimal under 1 with no leading 0, it will be multiplied by 100 and displayed as a percentage. To actually enter in a percentage less than 1 – 0.5% for example – you only need to add a leading 0. So 32 and .32 will both be displayed as 32.00%, but 0.32 will be displayed as 0.32%. **Scientific** displays a number in standard scientific notation, as a single digit plus two decimal places to an appropriate power – i.e. 65536 become 6.55E+04, read as "6.55 times 10 to the power of 4". As with Number, decimal places that are not displayed are still remembered. **Fraction** displays decimals as a standard fraction of up to three digits above and below the line – i.e. 0.14159264 displays as 16/113.

CHOOSING DATA TYPES

Getting Excel to pick a data type you want is simple. If you enter information into a cell in such a way that it looks like a particular data type, Excel will assign that data type to the cell. For example, if you type in 25%, the cell will become Percentage; if you type in 4 3/6, it will become Fraction. However, sometimes the program will choose a data type that you did not want – if you enter 1/4 for example, this will be converted to the date for April 1st, rather than to a fraction. There are two ways around this. You can force Excel to treat the cell as text by starting your information with a ' sign, as described earlier, or you can choose a new cell type manually:

1 Select the cell(s) to change type for by clicking on it. If it is already being edited or typed in (i.e. it has a thin black line around it), click on a different cell then click back on the first one, so that it has a thick black line around it.

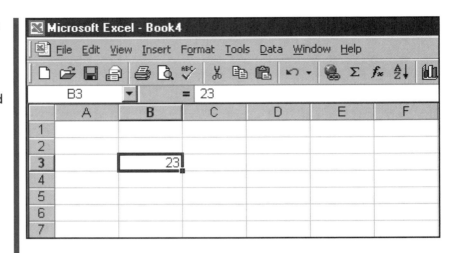

2 From the <u>Format</u> menu, choose the <u>Cells...</u> option

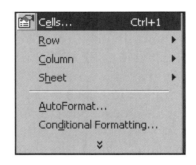

3 In the <u>Format Cells</u> dialog box, activate the <u>Number</u> tab (it is the default option) and double-click on the new type for the cell. The dialogue box will close, and the cell type will be changed.

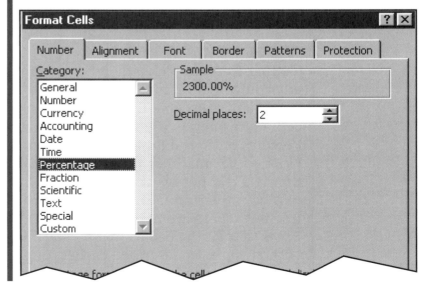

SPECIAL DATA TYPES

In addition to the standard data types, there are several extra data types provided by Excel. These are within the <u>Special</u> category. **Zip Code** presents a number as a standard American five-digit zip code – i.e. 90210 – and **Zip Code +4** works as a nine-digit zip code – i.e. 90210-4055. **Phone Number** presents the number as a standard American telephone code – i.e. (312) 555-7752. Finally, **Social Security Number** presents the data as a standard American SSN code – i.e. 334-22-7633. Obviously, these special data types are of limited use outside of the USA.

DEFINING NEW DATA TYPES

You can also use the Format Cells dialog box to create new data types of your own for handling numbers in a special way.

1 In the <u>Number</u> tab of the <u>Format Cells</u> dialogue box, click on <u>Custom</u>. The right-hand side of the dialogue box will display a <u>Type</u> list of format codes.

2 Choose a format code that you want to base your new data type on, and it will appear in the top bar of the Type list for you to edit.

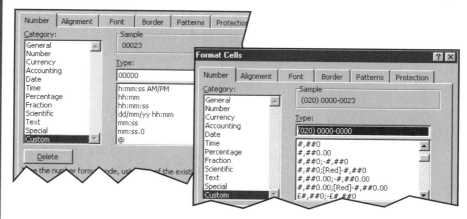

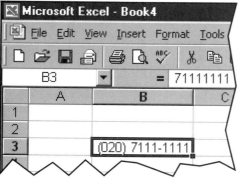

3 Edit the format code to define your new type. In the code, a '#' means "put a number here if there is one", a number (e.g. 0) means "always put a number here and fill this space with a 0 if there is not one", a ";" indicates an alternative option for display, and most other characters will just appear as typed. Once you are happy with your new format code – (020) 0000-0000 would give you a custom type for London, UK phone numbers – click <u>OK</u> and the cell will be formatted according to your new settings. Your custom data type will also be added to the bottom of the codes in the Type list, so you can use it again.

CELL RANGES

Much of the time, you will want to work with more than one cell at once. A lot of Excel's power comes from the way that you can select and manipulate whole ranges of cells at the same time, performing calculations on them or collecting them together into one big cell for visual effect. Mastering cell ranges is an extremely important part of getting the most from Excel.

SELECTING CELL RANGES

At its simplest, selecting many cells is very similar to selecting a single cell. Click on an inactive cell and, holding the mouse button down, drag the pointer to the opposite corner of the end you want to select. You can achieve the same effect by clicking on the start cell in the range, then holding down <u>Shift</u> and clicking on the last cell in the range.

1 Select multiple cells in a line using the mouse.

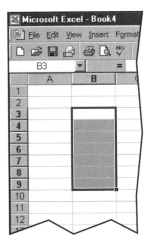

2 Select scattered cells using the mouse and the Ctrl key. Hold the Ctrl key down and click on each cell you wish to select, no matter where it lies on the spreadsheet.

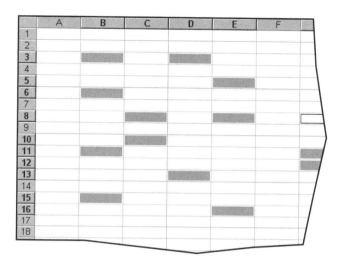

SCATTERED CELLS

You can simultaneously select cells that do not lie in a neat block with the aid of the Ctrl key. If you want to de-select the cells, just release the Ctrl key and click on any unselected cell.

SCATTERED RANGES

You can combine both of the above methods to select several ranges that do not link to form a block. Holding the Ctrl key down, you can click and drag to select a range as described on page 32, and then click and drag in a different place to select a subsequent range. You can also click on individual cells, and have them added to the group selection. A little keyboard kung-fu is necessary to manually select separate ranges with the Shift and Ctrl keys, but this can be very useful.

3 Select scattered ranges and single cells using a combination of methods.

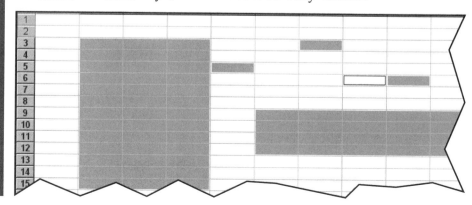

SELECTING ROWS AND COLUMNS

Aside from manually selecting ranges of cells, it is possible to select an entire column or row. The biggest single advantage of this is that the columns and rows are flexible in length. The columns descend vertically, are named by letter along the top, and go from A to Z and then, by default, from AA–AZ, and on through BA to IV. The rows spread across horizontally, are numbered down the side, and start at 1, going on down to row 65536 by default. If you select a range of cells with the mouse, you will only affect the cells you have chosen. Selecting an entire column or row (to set as a particular Data Type, for example) will provide you with as many cells as you could need. To select a column or row of cells, you click on the grey title block at the head of that column or row.

You can select a range of columns or a range of rows in the same way that you would select a range of cells, by dragging the mouse or shift-clicking, and you can select scattered columns and rows with the aid of the <u>Ctrl</u> button.

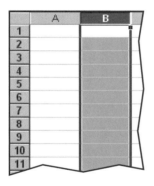

3 Select whole rows and columns by clicking on their grey title blocks.

SELECTING EVERYTHING

If you want to select all the cells in the entire worksheet, you just have to click once on the small, unmarked grey block where the column titles and row titles meet, in the very top left of the worksheet.

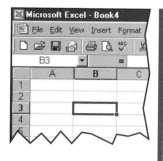

NAMING CELLS

Sometimes, you will need to refer to a cell by name. This can be handy if you want to tell someone where to look on a sheet, but its main use is in writing formulas that need to analyse cells (or cell ranges) on the worksheet. Formulas are mentioned on page 38, and will be convered in much greater detail later on, but for the moment you just need to know how cells are named, so that you can work with them later.

Individual cells are named by column first and then row. This system is simple and easy to understand. In the diagram top left, the selected cell is called B3. Its name can be seen in the box to the left of the formula bar at the top of the sheet.

A range of cells is named in a very similar manner, by the cell in the top left corner and then the cell in the bottom right corner, with the two cells separated by a colon. The range in the diagram left is called B3:H15. Note that the other possible names, H3:B15, H15:B3 and B15:H3, are not used.

If you want to refer to a number of ranges, they are generally shown as being separated by commas, as in the scattered range B3:C12,E5:J9,G14 below. You can also refer to an entire row or column by using just that part of the name and describing it as a range – Row 6 is 6:6 for example; Columns B and C are B:C.

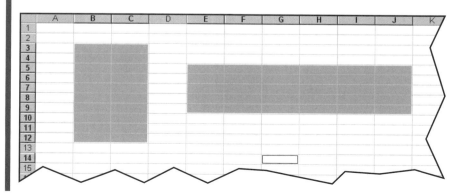

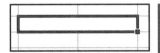

A merged cell.

MERGING CELLS

Sometimes, you will want to have access to a single cell that stretches several rows or columns, usually to enhance design or visual appeal. This is achieved by a process known as **merging**. When cells are merged, their internal borders are removed entirely, and they are then treated as if they were one large cell. The group is named after its top left cell, and data within the group is also treated as being inside that cell. Also note that if more than one cell in the merge holds data before you merge it, only the upper-leftmost piece of data will be saved in the merge. A merged cell has to be made of one single, continuous range. Merging a cell is simple.

1 Select the range of cells to merge.

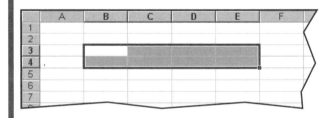

2 From the Format menu, choose the Cells... option

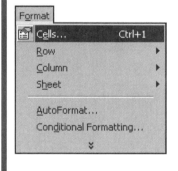

3 In the Format Cells dialog box, activate the Alignment tab. Towards the bottom left of the dialog box, you will see a tick-box labelled Merge cells. Select this tick box and click OK.

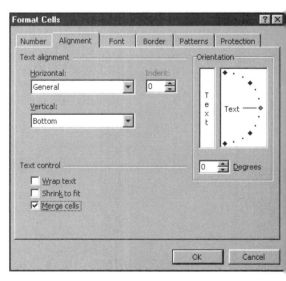

UNMERGING CELLS

When you unmerge a merged cell, all the cells in that group are returned back to being separate. Any data in the merged cell will be preserved in the upper-leftmost cell of the range, but all cell formatting will still apply to the whole range of cells. If you merged a range that included merged cells, those earlier merges are also undone.

1 Select the range of cells to unmerge.

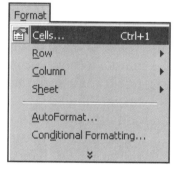

2 From the <u>Format</u> menu, choose the <u>Cells...</u> option

3 In the <u>Format</u> <u>Cells</u> dialog box, activate the <u>Alignment</u> tab. Deselect the <u>Merge</u> <u>Cells</u> tick box and click <u>OK</u>.

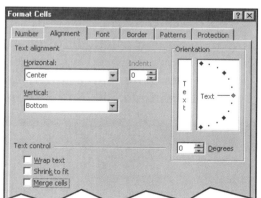

4 The merged cells will revert to being a selected range.

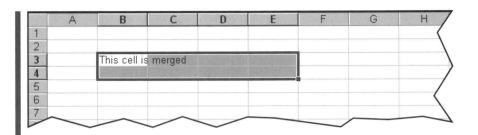

RELATIVE AND ABSOLUTE CELL REFERENCES

When you enter a formula, it is stored in a cell. Most formulas refer to other cells, known as target cells. By default, the names of the target cells are converted into a description of how far away the the target cell is from the cell that holds the formula. For example, if a formula in B3 refers to a target cell of A2, Excel will remember that target as being one left and one up. This is called Relative referencing. It has one very important implication – if you copy and paste the formula, the target will still be stored as one left and one up. If you copy and paste your formula from B3 to B4, one left and one up is now A3, not A2. That can make or ruin the formula's effects.

The way to avoid this problem is to use the cell's Absolute name. When you use a cell's Absolute name, the formula does not translate the name, and keeps it as the correct name of the target. That way, copying and pasting the formula from cell to cell will allow it to still refer to the original target cell. To make a cell's name absolute, add a dollar sign before each part of the name – for example, B3's absolute name is B3.

You can also provide a Mixed reference for a formula. This is useful for instances where you want to perform a number of similar calculations on different cells within one column or row. A mixed reference has one part of the name fixed as absolute with a $ sign, and the other part left relative – for example, $B3 and B$3 are both mixed references.

MERGING MERGES

You can also merge a range of cells that includes one or more merged cells itself, if you so wish. You can also perform a quick merge-and-center operation by clicking this icon (see image above left) on the task bar (or, if it isn't visible, from the <u>More Buttons</u> option at the end of the toolbar).

FORMATTING

There's a lot that you can do to make your Excel documents more effective and attractive. The program will let you change the way that data is displayed within cells, so that you can make important information stand out at a quick glance, or bring spreadsheets into line with in-house style. Similarly, you can change the way that the cells themselves appear, and even modify the appearance of the entire worksheet. This chapter will show you how.

3

FORMATTING DATA

The first place to begin learning about changing the appearance of your Excel worksheets is the way that the data itself is displayed in a cell. There are many different things you can do to the information inside a cell. Some of these are found in all good word processors, while others are a lot less common.

CHANGING FONT

The most basic piece of styling information is the font that the text is displayed in. A font is one set of letters and numbers with a consistent look and feel. To change font, either select the cell/s you want to change, or, if the cell is active, highlight the letters you want to change. Once you have the data selected, click on down arrow at the edge of the <u>Font Name</u> box, shown on the following page. Scroll through the list of fonts until you find the one you want, and then click on it. It will be selected, and the data's font will change.

CHANGING FONT STYLES

The box and three icons immediately to the right of the <u>Font Name</u> box are used for changing certain aspects of the way that your data is displayed. These are known as different styles of the basic font.

Normal text – the way that this sentence is displayed – is known as Roman, and it is the conventional form of showing printed text. The most common alternatives are to use a bold piece of text like **this**, or to set text as *italics* like this. Both are used to draw attention to information; bold text usually means

This is a Serif font, which has lines to terminate letter strokes.

This is a Sans Serif font, which has no lines to terminate letter strokes.

1 Click on the Fonts dropdown menu to be offered a choice of different fonts.

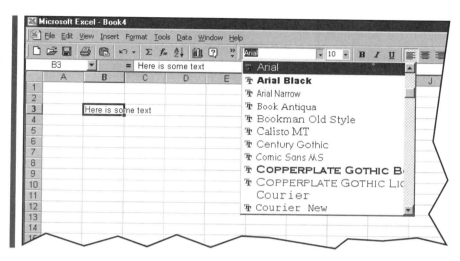

2 Use the options to the right of the font menu to change the appearance of your chosen font.

something is important or particularly significant, while italics usually means something is explanatory or should be spoken with emphasis. These rules vary, though. A fourth option is to combine both as bold italics, like *this*. This is less common, though. With the third icon, you can also choose to underline a piece of text like this, including bold, italics and bold italics. Simply select the cells or text that you want to modify, and click on one or more of the Bold, Italic or Underline icons shown above

The other basic change you can make to your normal font style is to alter the size of the letters themselves, called the point size, abbreviated to pt. The smaller the point size, the smaller the letters are. For easy reading, most normal text is displayed between 8pt – which looks like this – and 14pt – which looks like this. Headings and posters of course can be much, much larger, and legal text can be much smaller. Select the cells or text you want to modify, and use the **Point Size** box shown above – either click on it and type in your new point size between 1pt and 409pt, or click on the down-arrow and select a new point size from the drop-down list.

FONT EFFECTS

There are several other effects you can easily apply to your text.

1 Select the text or cells that you wish to apply an effect to.

2 From the Format menu, select Cells..., the first option. The Cell Format dialogue box will appear.

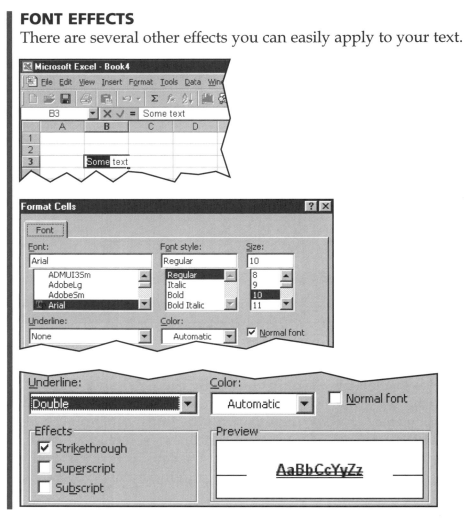

3 In addition to menus for font, font style, size and underline, you also have three buttons for effects, Strikethrough, Superscript and Subscript, and a text colour box which will give you a palette of colours you can choose from (by clicking) when you select it. You may choose any of these options for your text. When you are happy, click OK.

To give you an idea of what the different options look like, ~~this is 12pt Strikethrough~~, this is 12pt Superscript, this is 12pt Subscript, <u>this is underlined</u>, and this is coloured grey.

TEXT ALIGNMENT

There are several ways that Excel can position text within a cell. The way that the text is placed in relation to the borders of the cell is called alignment. As it has to apply to all the data within a cell, the alignment functions are not found on the <u>Font</u> tab of the <u>Cell Format</u> dialog box. However, the most common alignments have handy short-cut icons on the toolbar, found just to the right of the to the basic font style icons. The three most common ways of arranging text are as follows:

This is left-justified text, where the left side of the text is in a line along the left-hand edge, and the right-hand side is left to break naturally.

Its icon is:

This is centred text, where the lines are lined up with an even amount of space on both the left and right sides.

Its icon is:

This is right-justified text, the opposite of left-justified, where the right side of the text is lined up along the right edge, and the left-hand side is ragged.

Its icon is:

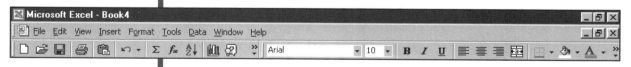

1 The alignment options are found to the right of the text formatting buttons.

All you have to do to select one of these options for the text in a cell is to select the text and click on the relevant icon in the toolbar (as shown above). This is the quickest method of changing the alignment. The alternative is to use the font dialog box, shown on the previous page. This allows you to change the alignment when you select the font.

OTHER ALIGNMENT OPTIONS

From the Alignment tab of the Format Cell dialog box, you can perform several advanced functions for aligning the text within one or more cells you have selected.

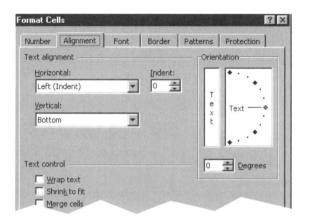  

If you click on the Horizontal or Vertical boxes, you'll see a list of possible alignment options as shown above. In the Horizontal box, Left (Indent), Center and Right are the options we discussed on the previous page. General means that the cell arranges text as left aligned, and numbers as right aligned – this is the default setting. Fill means that if the data in the cell is too long to fit inside, rather than displaying as spilling across empty cells, it will stop at the cell border. Justify works when Word Wrap is on (we'll talk about that next), and adds space between bits of data to make sure that both the left and right edges are in a straight line. Finally, Center Across Cells treats the position of your text as if the cells you have chosen were Merged, although they are not.

In the Vertical box, Top lines text up with the top edge of the cell, Center and Justify place it in the middle, and Bottom, the default, lines it up with the lower edge of the cell.

ADVANCED ALIGNMENTS

Sometimes, you may require a more sophisticated position for the data in a cell. Like all other text formatting and alignment matters, advanced alignments do not change the actual nature

1 Select advanced formatting options from the Format Cells dialog box.

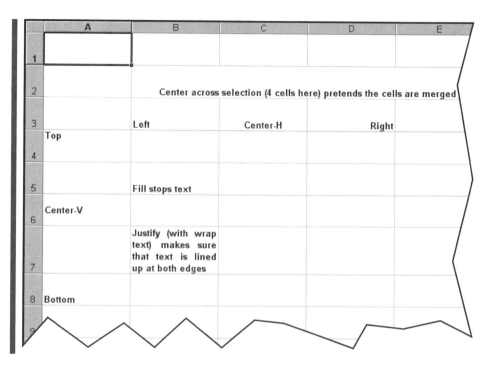

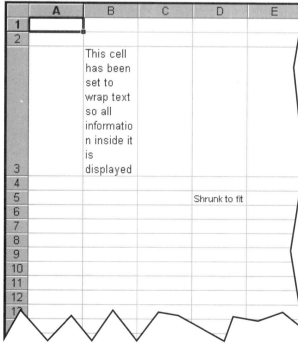

of the data in the cell, just its appearance. In the <u>Alignment</u> tab of the <u>Cell Format</u> dialogue box, there are three options under the heading of <u>Text Control</u> in the bottom left hand corner. <u>Merge Cells</u> was discussed on page 36. <u>Wrap Text</u> forces the cell to extend itself downwards, breaking the text into lines in order to fit its contents within the borders of the column. This extends the height of the whole row. <u>Shrink to Fit</u> has the opposite effect, reducing the point size of the contents of the cell so that all of the data is displayed within the cell's normal boundaries. If there is plenty of text, this can make it unreadable to the naked eye. Select the option you want and click <u>OK</u>.

FORMATTING CELLS

In addition to formatting the contents of a cell, it is also possible to format the cell itself. This allows you to perform a number of important tasks, not the least of which is protecting the contents of that cell from being changed. Other functions include changing the appearance of the cell, to make it more distinctive or to fit in with a particular style's needs.

BORDERS

Every cell is considered to have four borders, its top, bottom, left and right sides, known as the outsides. This is slightly more complicated when you select a number of cells; when a range is selected, the borders of the range itself are considered to be the outsides, and the lines between cells within the range, the internal horizontal and internal vertical lines, are known as the insides. Both inside and outside borders can be coloured so that they appear solid, and print as solid.

1 Select the cell or cells that you wish to apply an effect to.

2 From the FORMAT menu, select Cells.... Click on the Border tab and choose where you want the border, and which style and colour of line you want. For shading, click Patterns.

3 Clicking OK will add the border to your original selection.

4 If you wish to add a pattern, click on the Pattern tab inside the dialog. You will get a palette of colours and patterns. Change the colour of the pattern and select the shading style that you want from the Pattern dropdown menu.

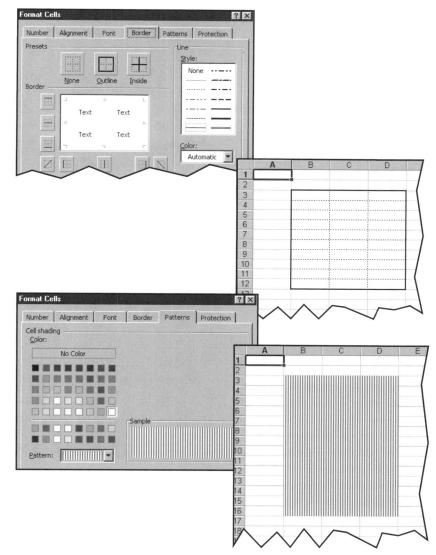

SHADING CELLS

You can easily colour a cell's background. Like other formats, this does not change the nature of the data, only the way that the cell appears on the screen and prints to paper. Shading refers to the basic colour of the cell background itself; patterning refers to a number of simple image patterns that can be applied to the cell background. A cell can be shaded, patterned or both shaded and patterned, and either aspect can be coloured.

CELL ORIENTATION

The <u>Orientation</u> sub-section of the <u>Cell Formatting</u> dialog box – which can be found on the right-hand side of the <u>Alignment</u> tab – allows you to change the angle that the contents of one or more cells are displayed at. Select the cells you want to modify, and call up the <u>Cell Formatting</u> dialog box from the <u>FORMAT</u> tool bar as usual. Click on <u>Alignment</u>.

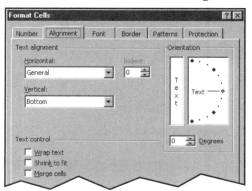

You click on the edges of the semi-circular <u>Orientation</u> diagram to position the text so that it reads at a different angle, anywhere from straight up to straight down (the font is twisted at an angle to match, as demonstrated within the Orientation preview box) or you can click on the vertical

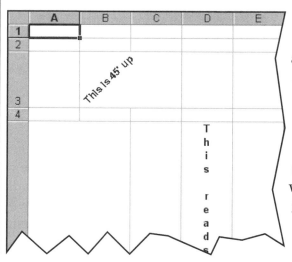

orientation image so that the text descends in a column. You can also type an angle from 90 to -90 into the <u>Degrees</u> box to choose an angle for displaying the cell contents. Simply select the option you want within the <u>Orientation</u> section and click <u>OK</u> for your text to be formatted.

CELL SIZE

It is possible to shrink or enlarge a cell as necessary. In fact, Excel will often do this automatically for one reason or another, such as to accommodate wrapped text, or to make room for text that is at a larger point size than normal. In addition, it is simple to change the size of the cells manually. You need to be aware however that because of the way Excel defines rows and columns, all the cells in one row have to be the same height, and all the cells in one column have to be the same width. If you increase the height and width of a cell, you will modify both the row and the column it is in.

SHRINKING AND ENLARGING

To enlarge or shrink a row, position the cursor at the bottom edge of the row you want to modify. The cursor will change to a cross-shaped image with up and down arrows. Click with the mouse, and drag the bottom edge of the row up or down as you require. Similarly, to enlarge or shrink a column, position the cursor at the right hand edge of the column you want to modify. The cursor will change to the cross-shape, with left and right arrows, and again you can click and drag to change the column size.

You can enter a precise size for a row or column by selecting the Row or Column submenu from the FORMAT toolbar as appropriate, and then select Height (for a Row) or Width (for a column). Enter the correct value and click OK. Finally, if you want to expand a row or column to exactly fit the size of a piece of data, the Autofit option on the Row and Column submenus will adjust the height or width as appropriate to fit to make sure the data fits inside the selected cell without wrapping or shrinking.

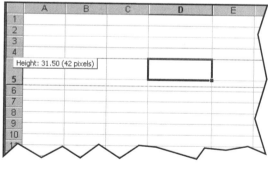

1 Change the size of cells by dragging their edges or by using the Row or Column heading from the FORMAT toolbar.

PROTECTING CELLS

Giving a cell protection means that it is no longer possible to change the contents of the cell until the protection is turned off. In addition, you can also set a cell to hide any formulas that it is storing, so that other people cannot see the calculation that is being performed. Locking or hiding a cell has no effect until you tell Excel to protect the sheet. Therefore, although when you start a new worksheet all the cells are locked by default, because the sheet is not protected, you can access all the cells as usual.

1 To turn work-sheet protection on, first select the TOOLS menu.

2 Go to Protection, so that the Protection sub-menu opens, and select the Protect Sheet option.

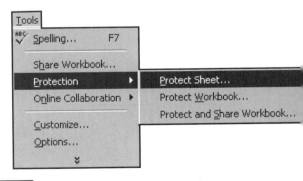

3 On the Protect Sheet dialogue box, ensure that the contents box is ticked. If you want to make sure that a password is required, type one into the password box. You will be asked for your password again. Click OK.

4 Now all cells set to be locked or hidden will be so. Unlock cells by repeating the process and clicking Unprotect.

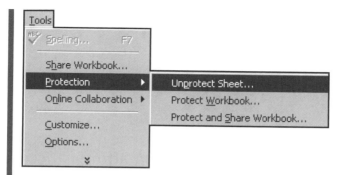

UNPROTECTING OR HIDING CELLS

You may want to unlock certain cells to allow them to have their contents modified at a later date once protection is in place. If the sheet is already protected, turn protection off. Select the cell or cells you wish to unprotect, which can even be the entire sheet if you wish, and then call up the Cell Format dialog box, from the Cells option on the FORMAT menu, and select the Protection tab. Click on the tick-box for Locked until it is empty, and click OK.

Similarly, if you want cell formulas hidden, select the cells and tick the Hidden box on the Protection tab. Once you have unlocked, hidden and/or unhidden the cells that you want to, and all your formatting is in place, you can protect the sheet. Only those cells you have specifically unlocked will be modifiable, and only to the extent that data can be entered into them.

1 Use the Format Cells dialog box to change the protection values of your cells or tables.

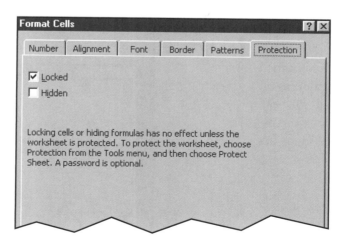

FORMATTING WORKSHEETS

Although most formatting is done at the level of cells or below, there are several options open to you when it comes to formatting an entire worksheet. These include hiding and unhiding entire rows and columns, adding a background to your worksheet, and setting conditional styling.

HIDING ROWS AND COLUMNS

When you hide a row or column, that entire selection of cells is no longer displayed. The information held within it is not lost, nor, to the program itself, is it moved in any way. The cells are still there… they just aren't shown on the screen. This can be useful if you want to include data for formulas to work on so that results can be seen, but you do not actually want the data itself to be accessible.

1 To hide a row or column, click on any cell/s within the row/s or column/s you want to hide, or alternatively click on the title block so the row/s or column/s are selected.

2 Go to the FORMAT menu, and click on either Row or Column depending on which you want to hide.

3 Click on Hide, and the row or column will be hidden.

4 To Unhide, reverse the process, and in the FORMAT menu, select the Row or Column sub-menu as appropriate, and click on Unhide.

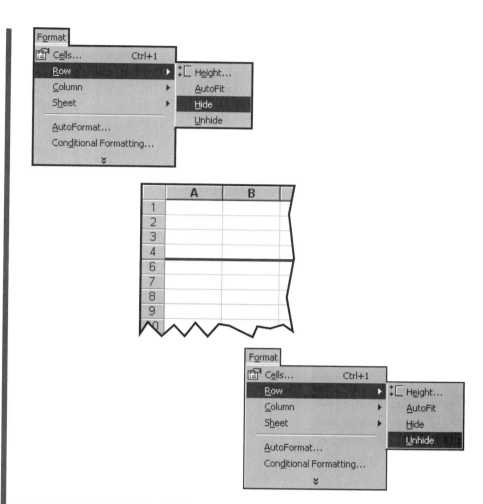

UNHIDING ROWS AND COLUMNS

Unhiding a row or column is only slightly more complex than hiding it in the first place. The basic idea is that, as when hiding a row or column, you select the item and then unhide it. However, because the item is no longer visible on the screen for you to select, you have to select it as part of range – in other words, you have to select a range that includes at least one cell from the items either side of the hidden one. So, if you have hidden Row 5 and want to get it back, you have to drag a range from Row 4 to Row 6. Then, a cell in Row 5 will also be selected, and you can unhide the row. Unhiding a column involves exactly the same process.

WORKSHEET BACKGROUNDS

Excel will readily allow you to add a graphical background image to your spreadsheet. You select a graphics file from disk, and the program places it on the screen at full size, if necessary repeating the image so that the screen is filled up. Your normal cells are then redrawn over the image. If a cell has a colour or pattern set, that will take priority over the background image, so that if your background makes text difficult to read, you can set the cell to have a white or other pale background, and its data will be easy to see again.

1 From the FORMAT menu, select the Sheet submenu, and click on the Background... option. This will open the Sheet Background dialog box.

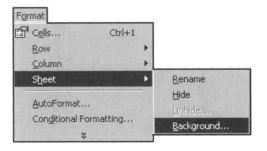

2 Move to the file you want to use as a background image, and select it. Click Insert.

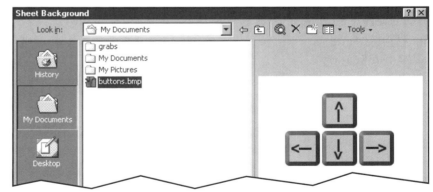

3 Your image will be tiled across the Excel window.

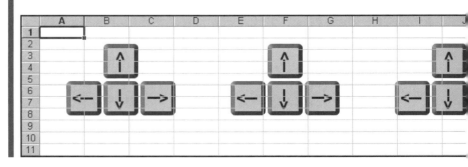

WHEN TO USE CONDITIONAL FORMATTING

Conditional Formatting is a process whereby a cell switches to a certain different style when a particular condition is met. You choose the conditions that will activate the special style, and you also define the special style's appearance. This makes it an extremely powerful and flexible tool. The main use for Conditional Formatting is for alerting you to special circumstances, such as mistakes, undesirable results, and other elements that you would like to make sure you become aware of immediately. Because it flags up errors, Conditional Formatting is also known as Trapping.

In the illustrations below, a set of cells at the top of the screen have been set to switch to a bright pattern when the profit box in Cell G15 falls below 20%. In the first example, that profit figure is higher, and the cells at the top of the screen are formatted normally; in the second example, the figure is lower, and the cells have switched formatting.

You can clearly see the difference between the two sheets. Above, row 1 is formatted normally, and right, the whole of row 1 is filled with a pattern, alerting you.

APPLYING A CONDITIONAL FORMAT
Setting one or more cells to change style conditionally is simple.

1 Select the cell or cells you wish to modify, and then choose Conditional Formatting... from the FORMAT menu.

2 The Conditional Formatting dialog box will appear. The default settings let you specify a value for the cell to fall between; to use this, just add the range value you want to be alerted to into the range boxes, either side of the word And. Note that some settings do not require a range – "not equal to" for example.

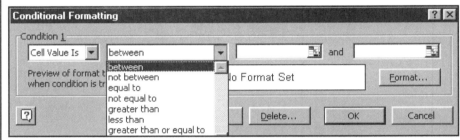

3 Once you have applied your conditions, you can select the new Cell style for the conditional format. Click the Format button to select styling options.

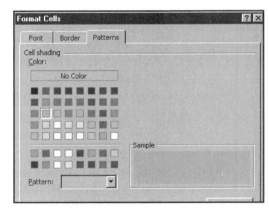

4 The Conditional Formatting dialog box will show the new conditional format. Click OK to activate the new settings.

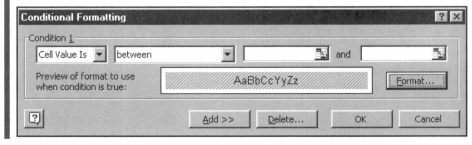

WORKING WITH DATA

4

There are many ways within Excel to manage your data and make it do what you want. In this chapter, we'll introduce you to the basics of making the most of your data, including how to get Excel to fill in the blanks for you, introducing you to simple formulas, working with lists and basic functions, and creating charts based on your data.

SERIES DATA

Excel is able to examine a range of cells, match their contents to one of a number of pre-set types of data – such as number series, times, sales quarters and so on – and then extend the range as you need, saving you lots and lots of typing. It can also perform other calculations on ranges of data, such as totalling them for you. In this section, we'll explore the basics of working with a series of data.

TYPES OF DATA SERIES

Excel understands several different types of series, most of which are numerical. The simplest is a standard arithmetical progression – 1, 2, 3…; 10, 20, 30…; 17, 34, 51… – which Excel can deduce from just two numbers. It also recognises days of the week (Mon, Tue as well as Monday, Tuesday), times in 12hr or 24hr format, dates, month names (as both Jan, Feb and January, February), and quarterly results, as Qtr 1 through Qtr 4, or as Quarter 1 through Quarter 4. It can also work with numbers set in any standard format, such as percentages, currencies and so on. If you add a number to a word – Jason 1, Jason 2, Jason 3 and so on – it will work with that number.

	A	B	C	D	E
1					
2		1	Monday	13:15	Qtr1
3		2	Tuesday	13:45	Qtr2
4		3	Wednesday	14:15	Qtr3
5		4	Thursday	14:45	Qtr4
6		5	Friday	15:15	Qtr1
7		6	Saturday	15:45	Qtr2
8		7	Sunday	16:15	Qtr3
9		8	Monday	16:45	Qtr4
10		9	Tuesday	17:15	Qtr1
11		10	Wednesday	17:45	Qtr2
12		11	Thursday	18:15	Qtr3
13		12	Friday	18:45	Qtr4
14		13	Saturday	19:15	Qtr1
15		14	Sunday	19:45	Qtr2
16					
17					
18					
19					

AUTOFILLING A DATA SERIES

1 Click and drag to autofill a simple data series.

The simplest way to get Excel to extend a series of data for you is to select the first two cells in the series as a range, and then click on the small black box in the bottom right corner of the selection outline – the pointer will turn into a + sign – and drag the range. Dragging down or to the right will increment – that is, increase – the data in the range; dragging up or to the left will decrement – decrease – it.

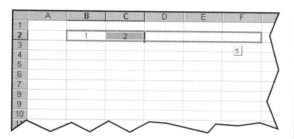

If you click and drag on the handle with the right mouse button, then when you release the button you will get a menu of fill options – <u>Fill Series</u> is the same as above, while <u>Copy Cells</u> just duplicates your original cells into the range in their entirety, <u>Fill Formats</u> copies cell formatting only from your original range, and <u>Fill Values</u> copies the data only. At the bottom, <u>Linear Trend</u> fills a numerical series in the normal way, while <u>Growth Trend</u> converts your data to a simple exponential curve similar to interest calculations, and fills based on that.

You can also select the Series… dialog box from the short-cut right-click menu, or from the <u>EDIT</u> menu, <u>Fill</u> submenu, <u>Series…</u> option, which will let you select certain advanced functions.

THE AUTOSUM FUNCTION

AutoSum is a version of the Sum Function that allows you to quickly total a range of figures. There are many functions, and we will discuss them in more detail later, but Sum is used . more than any other Function.

1 Click on the first empty cell at the end of the row or column, and click the AutoSum button in the menu bar.

2 The AutoSum function will automatically select the data series you are next to, surrounding it with a dotted line. If this is the correct data to add together, press Return.

3 The cell you originally selected will now hold the total, and will update itself to stay correct if you change the numbers it has added up.

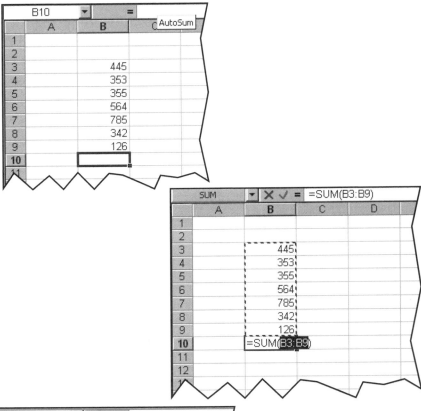

AN INTRODUCTION TO CELL FORMULAS

As we already discussed, every Cell and range can be referred to by name. Cells can be told to perform a calculation based on other cells, and this is called a formula. To tell Excel that you are giving a cell a formula, you start the data in that cell with an equals sign. The simplest formula of all is to tell the cell you are typing the formula into (the ORIGIN) to be the same as another cell (the TARGET). If you want to make your origin be the same as cell C1 (for example), the formula for that is simply =C1. You can use simple mathematical symbols, so =C1+C4-(D7*D8) is also a valid formula. As we discussed on the previous page, you can do a sum of a range, as in =SUM(C1:C8) and you can also include any other of Excel's built in Functions. We'll have a look at other Functions later on.

When you look at a cell holding a formula on the screen, only the formula's result will be displayed. To see the formula being used, select the cell. The formula will be displayed in the aptly-named <u>Formula Bar</u> towards the top of the screen. If the formula cannot be calculated, the cell will display an Error message starting with a # sign.

1 In this example, the result of a mathematical formula based on the numbers in A1 to A10 is displayed in A12. The total is displayed in the contents of cell A12 and the formula in the bar.

A12	▼	=	=A1-A2+A3-A4+A5-A6+A7-A8+A9-A10

	A	B	C	D	E	F	G
1	445						
2	353						
3	355						
4	564						
5	785						
6	342						
7	926						
8	257						
9	345						
10	188						
11							
12	1152						
13							
14							
15							
16							
17							

WORKING WITH LISTS

A data list is, put simply, a selection of standard headings – one to a column – known as a Header List, followed by a number of entry rows, each one storing information under most or all of the headings. There are many different situations where you might want to use a list of data, from storing addresses of friends or clients through to tracking sales figures. Lists are often used as the basic format of a database, and this will be discussed fully later on, but in this section we're going to introduce you to lists and some of the simple tasks that can be done with them.

	A13	▼	=						
	A	B	C	D	E	F	G	H	I
1	TITLE	INITIAL	SURNAME	HONORIFIC	COMPANY	ADDRESS1	ADDRESS2	TOWN	POSTCODE
2	Mr	G	Worksop	Dear Sir	Hungerford	15, The High Street		London	E1 3LA
3	Mr	J	Bowyer	Dear Sir	Alissa	Rathbone Market	Barking	London	E16 1RT
4	Mrs	D	Harper	Dear Madam	Phoenix Holdings	Hainault Road		London	E11 6TE
5	Ms	R	Jones	Dear Ms. Jones	Northern	Woodgrange Road		London	E7 6RG
6	Mr	T	Lightman	Dear Sir	Surma Co	Whitechapel High Street	Whitechapel	London	E1 D25
7	Mrs	O	Worne	Dear Madam	Richards Direct	Selborne Walk	Walthamstow	London	E17 8ED
8	Mr	W	Laidlaw	Dear Bill	Kenton	Somerset Road	Walthamstow	London	E17 8QR
9			The Manager	The Manager	Conant	Station Parade	Upper Clapton Rd	London	E5 3UJ
10	Mr	F	Yardley	Dear Sir	Fountain Times	Claremot Road		London	E17 4DC
11	Mrs	D	Williams	Dear Madam	Hairdays	Plashet Grove		London	E6 1AD
12	Mrs	T	Surne	Dear Tina	Bluesky	Station Road	Chingford	London	E3 7BU
13									
14									
15									
16									
17									
18									
19									
20									

This is the complete data list that we will be working from. It comprises names and addresses.

SORTING LIST DATA

Sorting is one of the most useful functions that a list will allow you to perform. By grouping different pieces of information together, you can get access to all sorts of facts. For example, grouping a client list by postcode or city will let you find everyone in an area, which can help you to arrange business trips. You can also sort according to a specific type of data, arranging days of the week in date order rather than in strict alphabetical order, for example.

1 To sort a list, first select your entire data list. Make sure that your row of column headings is the first selected row.

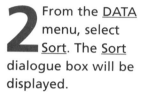

2 From the DATA menu, select Sort. The Sort dialogue box will be displayed.

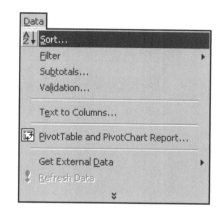

3 Make sure the Header Row radio button at the bottom of the Sort dialog is selected, then click on the top box, titled Sort By. Select the heading you want to sort by. Ascending sorts in normal alphabetical or numerical order, and Descending sorts backwards.

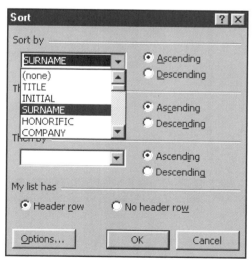

4 If you want to fine-tune your sort by performing a second or third sort, select the headers in the <u>Then By</u> boxes. For example, you could sort by town, and then by company.

5 You can tell Excel to compare data in your table to one of your data types. Click the <u>Options</u> box, and then click on the <u>First key sort order</u> box. Select from a list of data types in that box, and click <u>OK</u>.

6 If you select a column that contains some of your chosen data type, entries that match that type will be sorted into type order first.

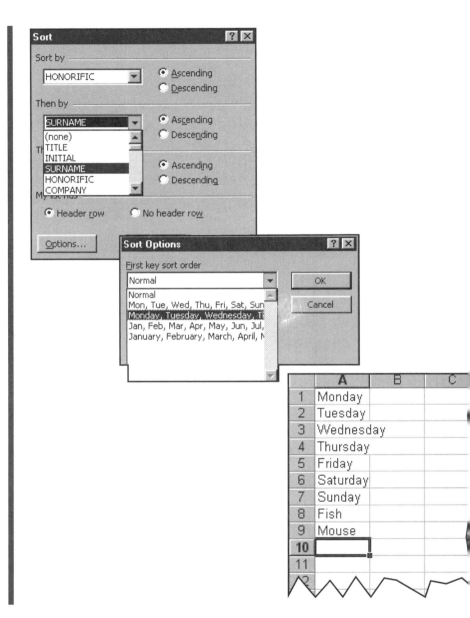

CREATING NEW DATA TYPES

Given that data types are such an important and integral part of working effectively with lists, it is useful to know how to create a new type. For example, product codes often change over time in a way that is not directly alphabetical, and it can be useful to sort them by age, so a data type that puts those product codes in order (such as ALx, BEx, UNx, ARx, REx, ANx, etc.) can provide you with a handy tool. Additionally, new data types will allow you to swiftly create an Autofill list based on that type, as discussed earlier.

1 From the TOOLS menu, select Options.

2 The Options dialog box will appear. Click on the tab marked Custom Lists.

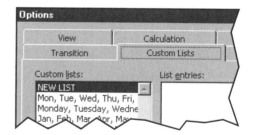

3 Ensure the NEW LIST option is selected in the Custom Lists box, and then enter your new data type items, in the order you want them to sort. You should press Return after each new item. When your new data type is finished, click Add. The new data type will be displayed in the Custom Lists: box. Click OK to finish.

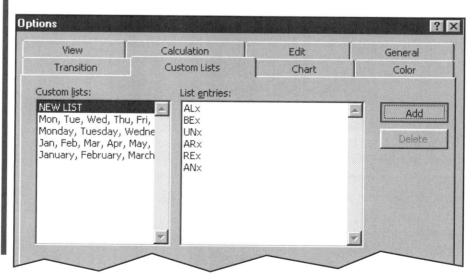

CREATING A NEW DATA TYPE FROM A CELL RANGE

If you have already entered a list of data that you would like to turn into a new data type, you do not have to type all the information into the <u>List Entries</u> box when starting a new type.

1 Select one range of data, part of either one column or one row. This range should hold the data that you wish to make into the new data type, one item to a cell.

2 Call up the <u>Options</u> dialog from the <u>TOOLS</u> menu and select the <u>Custom Lists</u> tab. The <u>Import List From Cells</u> box will hold the absolute names of your selected cell range.

3 Click the <u>Import</u> box, and the entries will appear in both the <u>List Entries</u> box and the <u>Custom Lists</u> boxes as a new list. Click <u>OK</u> to close the dialog box.

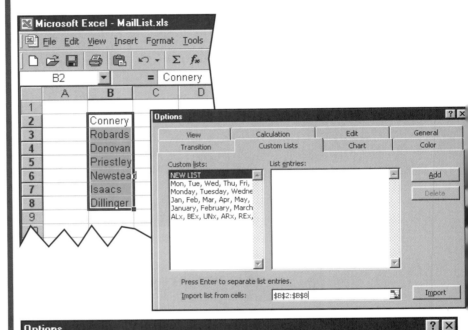

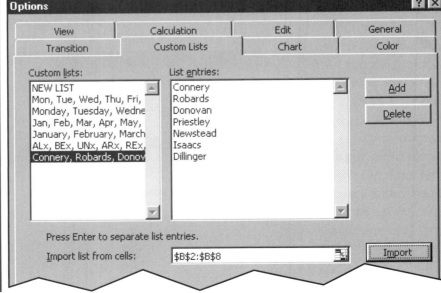

DE-DUPING A LIST

There are a few common tasks that are involved in managing a useful list of data. One of the most important of these is making sure that you do not have the same information duplicated across two or more entries – particularly vital if you plan to use your list to print envelopes or mailing labels, for example. The process of ensuring that each line of data is unique is called de-duping.

Unfortunately, it would take an Artificial Intelligence to automatically de-dupe a list. Despite seeming rather simple on the surface, it is in fact an extremely complicated task that requires the ability to spot underlying patterns and similarities in the language. That means that it has to be done manually – there is, as of yet, no computing substitute for human judgement and experience. Simple errors of spelling or differences in entered data can make it difficult to spot duplicates in one sweep, so you will probably need to sort your list by several different columns.

SORTING FIRST

To de-dupe a list, sort it by its most unique column – usually company name, post-code or surname. You will then need to read through all of the the entries, comparing each to the entries above and below it by eye. If they seem close enough to be the same information – you'll need to judge this based on your own list – click on one of the duplicated rows, and press <u>Delete</u> to empty it. Repeat this process for at least two and ideally three different sort criteria.

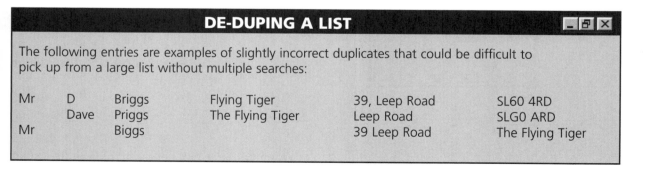

DE-DUPING A LIST

The following entries are examples of slightly incorrect duplicates that could be difficult to pick up from a large list without multiple searches:

Mr	D	Briggs	Flying Tiger	39, Leep Road	SL60 4RD
	Dave	Priggs	The Flying Tiger	Leep Road	SLG0 ARD
Mr		Biggs		39 Leep Road	The Flying Tiger

INTRODUCING CHARTS

The most effective way of demonstrating a trend in numerical data is to convert it into a chart. Charts are simple and eye-grabbing, and can make your point in the sort of punchy, effective way that a thousand words or a complicated spreadsheet could not. Excel has a built-in tool for making chart preparation really simple, called the Chart Wizard.

PREPARING YOUR CHART DATA

The first thing to do is to format the data that you want to represent graphically into a range. The most common way of doing this is to prepare it as a mini-list, with one or more headings, and the appropriate data underneath it. Different types of chart are appropriate for different amounts of data. If you want to plot a graph of data, then you will want two or three sets of data points; if you want to plot a pie chart, you will want only one set of values, but each may require a heading. Once you have prepared the data you want to depict, you need to select it as a range.

A small selected range, ready to generate a chart.

STARTING THE CHART WIZARD

With the range of data that you want to base your chart on selected, click on the Chart Wizard icon on the toolbar.

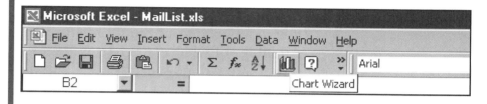

Use <u>Chart</u> in the <u>INSERT</u> menu.

SELECTING A CHART TYPE

In either case above, the Chart Wizard (pictured below) will start up and you will be presented with a list of chart types to select from. Click on the icons in the <u>Chart Type</u> list to the left to select a basic style of chart, and different variations on that theme will be displayed in the <u>Chart Sub-type</u> box on the right. At the bottom of the sub-type box, a small description of what that type of chart is used for is displayed. When you are happy with your selected chart type, click <u>Next></u>.

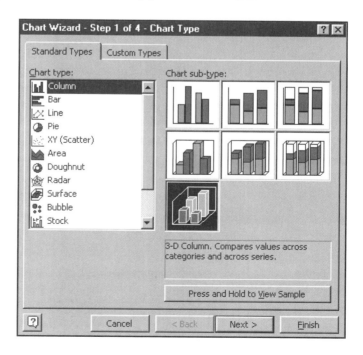

1 Start generating your chart with the <u>Chart Wizard</u>. In Setp 1 you select your chart style.

SOURCING CHART DATA

By default, the Chart Wizard will use the range of data that you have highlighted to form the chart and label its axes. Its selections will be shown in the <u>Chart Source Data</u> dialogue of the <u>Chart Wizard</u>, the second step. If the wizard has misunderstood your requirements, you can correct that here. An image of what your chart will look like is shown in the center of the dialogue, complete with labels. You can change the orientation of your data range by clicking on the <u>Rows</u> and <u>Columns</u> radio buttons. The sample will update.

2 Make sure that Excel is using the correct data to generate your chart in the <u>Data Range</u> tab.

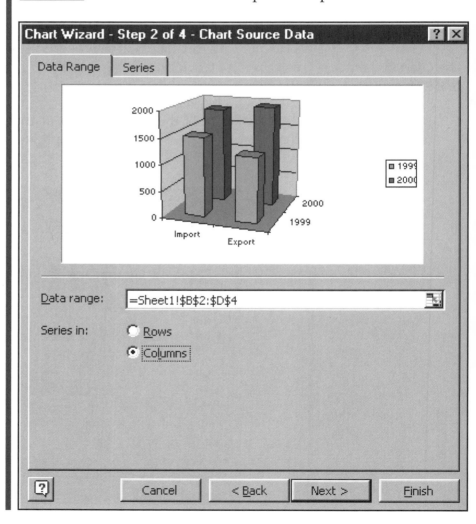

If you want to be specific about the locations of your data, click on the Series tab and then on the name of the data series you want to modify. If you then alter the absolute addresses that the wizard is using for that data, you will change the data accordingly. You can also click Add to create a new data series that is not referenced on the chart, and type its name into the Name box, and its values, seperated by commas, into the Value box. When you're happy you have the right data, click Next> to continue to the next stage.

3 Adjust the data Series that the Wizard is using, if you need to.

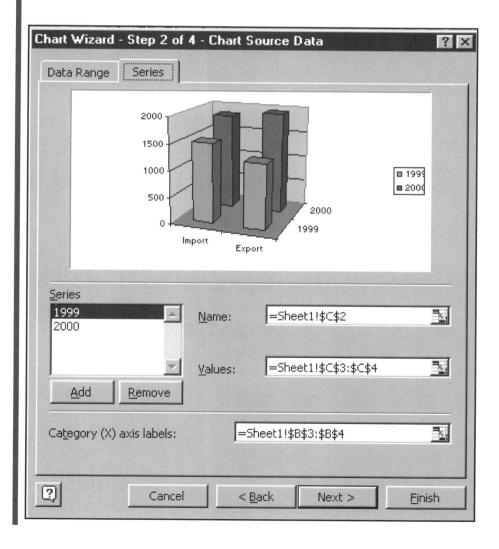

CHART OPTIONS

There are several additional pieces of information that you can add in to the chart, to clarify your data. All of these are entered in Step 3 of the Chart Wizard, the Chart Options dialog. The Chart Options dialog has six tabs, Titles, Axes, Gridlines, Legend, Data Labels, and Data Table. Each of these allows you to make a different modification, and shows you a preview of your final chart. You should be aware that the more explanatory information you add to the chart, the smaller a space your final chart will be given.

4 You can fully tailor the way your chart will be presented in Step 3 – Chart Options.

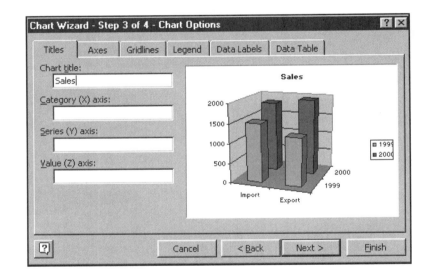

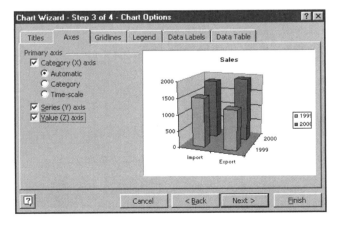

Titles allows you to add explanatory labels to the chart and its axes, so that all the information is clear. Whatever you type in is added to your preview.

Axes lets you specify whether or not the axis names you specified in your data range are included or not and, in some cases, what format that name takes.

Gridlines provides you with the option of specifying whether or not the chart displays grid bars – major lines

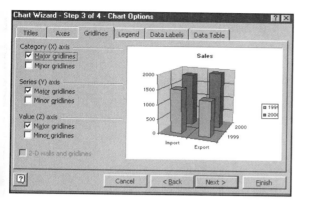

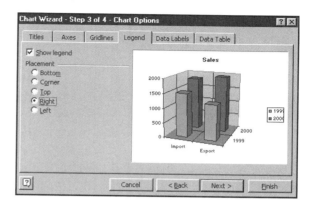

show the division between series or, for values, major marker points, while minor lines include smaller, more regular spacing.

Legend lets you choose whether or not a box showing the different chart colours and patterns are listed with an explanation of what they stand for, and where the box itself is placed.

Data Labels provides you with the option of showing the exact value of each entry on the chart as a piece of text attached to that chart, and if this is selected, showing the appropriate legend colour with the text.

Data Table allows you to include the information that went into making up the chart along with the chart itself, as part of its body. This can also be augmented with coloured Legend labels.

When you are happy with the look of your chart as it appears in the preview, click Next>.

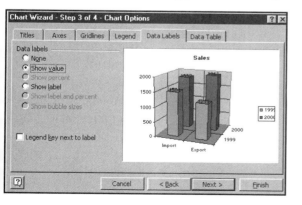

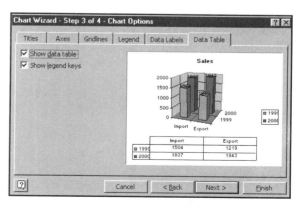

5 Make sure you know where your chart will be displayed, and click on <u>Finish</u> to generate your chart.

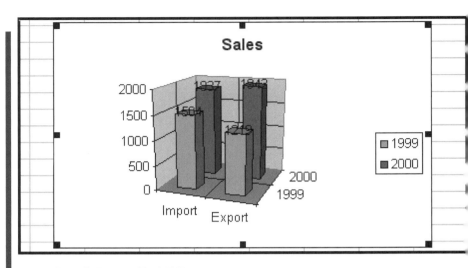

PLACING THE CHART

The final stage of the Chart Wizard allows you to choose whether to put your new chart into a currently existing worksheet – the lower of the two options, but also the default one – or as a new worksheet. Select whichever option you prefer, and click <u>OK</u>. The chart will be finished and placed.

MOVING AND SIZING

We'll look into some of the ways that you can customize the appearance of your chart later using the <u>Chart</u> toolbar that appears whenever your chart is selected, but for the moment we'll just consider how to move and re-size it. To change the placing of your chart on the worksheet, click on the border of the box that holds the chart and drag it. The pointer changes to a cross, and you will be able to move the chart around as an outline.

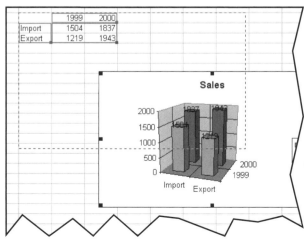

6 To resize your chart, make sure it is selected, and then click on one of the eight handles around the chart border. Drag that handle in or out to resize the chart from that side or corner.

FINISHING TOUCHES

5

Once you've got your Excel sheet looking right, there are a few other bits and pieces that are going to be useful. You might want to work with a second sheet for a while, in which case knowing how to find your way around a workbook is going to be useful. It is also important to know how to go about printing the work you have done – and how to check what it looks like before you do, so you don't waste time and paper – and how to get information from Microsoft's built in help system.

DIFFERENT VIEWS

There are several different methods with which you can modify the way Excel shows you the worksheet, and these will be of use to you at a variety of different times. This section will explore various ways of looking at your work.

ZOOM

The most basic method of changing the appearance of your worksheet on the screen is with the Zoom function. This changes the size that your data is displayed at. You may need to enlarge the view if you are working with cells that contain data displayed at a small point size, or to closely examine graphics, while you may need to shrink the view if you want to consider page layout issues and check the positioning and overall impact of formatting.

1 To change the display ratio, select Zoom... from the VIEW menu.

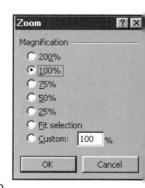

2 The Zoom dialog box will be displayed. Click on the magnification that you would like or if you have a range selected that you want to fill the screen with, click on Fit Selection.

3 Click <u>OK</u>, and your new magnification will be displayed, in this example, 400%.

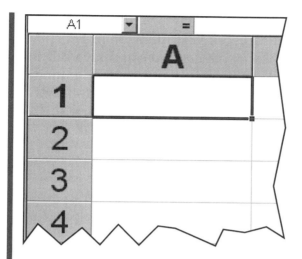

DIFFERENT WORKSHEETS

Excel allows you to work on more than one sheet at a time. You can use different sheets for different parts of your work, such as entering raw data onto one sheet, entering a list of information onto a second one, and then bringing totals and excerpts from them together on a third sheet. You can add an absolute sheet name – such as <u>Sheet1</u>! – to a cell reference in order to make sure that it is the right sheet's cell that is used in a calculation, comparison, formula or other item. The full absolute name for the first cell of the first sheet is Sheet1!A1.

ADDING A NEW SHEET

Excel starts you off with three sheets in a workbook, which is generally sufficient, but if you want a new sheet added to the ones you already have, choose the option <u>Worksheet</u> from the <u>INSERT</u> menu. A tab for the new sheet will be displayed at the bottom of the screen. You can change the order that the tabs are in by clicking on the tab you wish to move and dragging it to a new position in the row.

VIEW PANES

You can split your view of an Excel Worksheet into sections, known as panes, that can display different parts of the worksheet. This is primarily intended to let you keep header lines or other informational rows and columns visible while scrolling through extended panels of data.

1 To split your view window into panes, you can either double-click or click and drag on the Horizontal and/or Vertical Split Box...

2 ...or to do both splits at once, you can select <u>Split Panes</u> from the <u>WINDOW</u> menu.

3 Vertical split panes can show you different columns but the same rows, while horizontal split panes can show you different rows but the same columns.

4 Keep or change your selection by using <u>Freeze Panes</u> and <u>Unfreeze Panes</u> from the Window menu.

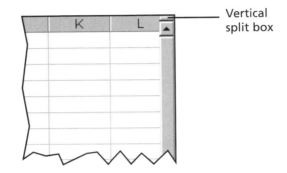

Vertical split box

Horizontal split pane

Vertical split pane

MULTIPLE WORKBOOKS

You can work with multiple workbooks – that is, with multiple Excel files – at the same time. Individual sheets can be moved or copied from one workbook to another as easily as they can be moved inside one workbook:

2 The Move or Copy dialog will appear. Select the name of the active workbook you want to move the sheet to (the default is to stay within the same workbook) from the To Book list.

3 Select the position that the new sheet is to be placed in the workbook you have chosen by selecting the sheet it is to appear before from the list in the Before Sheet box.

4 If you want to copy the sheet, tick the Create A Copy box in the bottom left, or to move it, untick it. Click OK and the sheet will be copied or moved.

1 With the sheet you want to move or copy active, select the Move or Copy Sheet command from the EDIT menu.

ARRANGING WINDOWS

To allocate equal space to the workbooks you have open within Excel, click on the Arrange... option in the Windows menu. From the Arrange Windows dialogue that appears, select one of the four different options for arranging your different workbooks, make sure the Windows of Active Workbook box is unticked, and click OK.

PRINTING YOUR WORK

In many instances, it is going to be important to get a paper copy of your worksheet. Even if a document is never to be distributed or filed, a paper copy to refer to will aid you while you work, and give you a clearer image of the overall presentation of your work than an on-screen view. In this section, we will look at how to prepare a worksheet for printing.

PRINT PREVIEW

The most useful tool for making sure that a printed copy of your worksheet turns out as expected is the Print Preview. From the <u>FILE</u> menu, select <u>Print Preview</u>. The screen switches to Print Preview mode. This will show you what Excel is going to send to the printer, page by page. Clicking on <u>Margins</u> will show you where the margins of the page are and where the different row and column lines are, and you can drag all these elements and move them around to make the document look better. You can return to normal view by clicking <u>Close</u>.

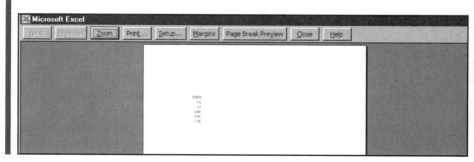

PRINTING AN AREA

If you want to print just a sub-section of your worksheet, it is easy to set this up as the only area that will be printed.

1 Select the range of cells that you want to print. This has to be one continuous range. To include a chart or other graphical addition in the print area, all the cells around its borders have to be included in the range.

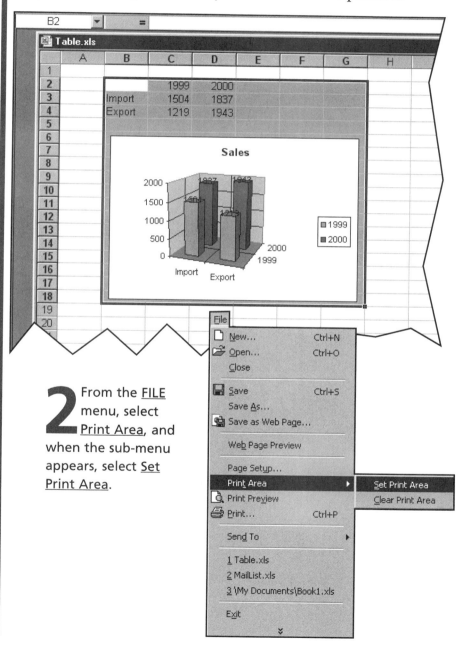

2 From the FILE menu, select Print Area, and when the sub-menu appears, select Set Print Area.

3 The menu will close, and the range you have selected will be surrounded by a dotted line. This dotted area will now be the only cells that will print, as you can verify with the Print Preview function.

4 To return the sheet to printing in its entirity, go to Print Area in the FILE menu, and select Clear Print Area. The sheet will return to normal.

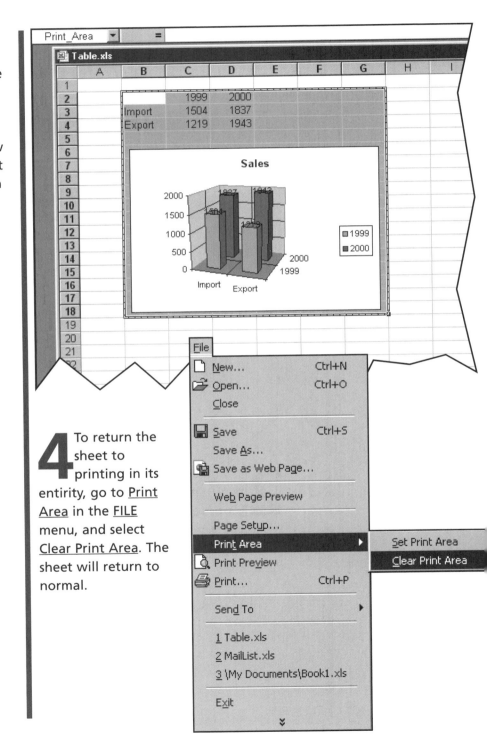

PRINTING

When you are ready to print, and the Print Preview shows that things are arranged to your satisfaction, select <u>Print...</u> from the <u>FILE</u> menu. The <u>Print</u> dialog box will appear:

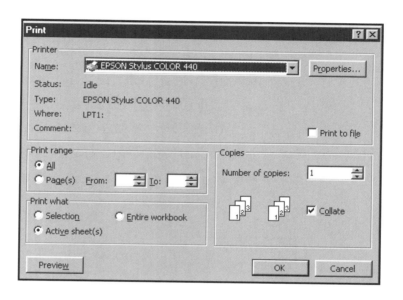

The <u>Print Range</u> area of the dialog tells the printer which pages to print from your document. To print a sub-section, click on <u>Page(s)</u> and then enter the range of pages to print. The <u>Print What</u> area defines the extent of your printing – either all the content of the current worksheet (the default setting, called <u>Active Sheet</u>), all the content from all worksheets in the workbook (<u>Entire Workbook</u>), or just the range you currently have selected (<u>Selection</u>). In the <u>Copies</u> area, you can define how many copies of your data Excel will print – just alter the number in the <u>Number of Copies</u> box. If <u>Collate</u> is ticked, copies will be printed as entire sets of the document, one after another; if it is unticked, each page will print all its copies before moving on to the next page. The image to the left of the <u>Collate</u> box demonstrates this. The <u>Printer</u> area of the <u>Print</u> dialog is fairly advanced, so only modify it if you know what you are doing.

Getting Help

Excel, like all of the Microsoft Office, comes with several useful help features built in, including the popular Office Assistant. This animated character sits in the bottom right hand corner of your screen, and provides you with help when you click on it.

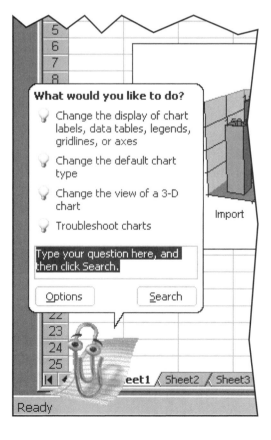

THE OFFICE ASSISTANT

There are several different characters you can choose from, set up when the program is installed. When you click on the Assistant, it will attempt to work out what you are doing at that time, and offer help on it. It will also ask questions whenever Excel needs to know a piece of information.

If one of the options it presents seems to be able to assist you, click on it and detailed help will be displayed. If none of them do, type a question in the box marked Type A Question Here, and click Search. You can turn the Assistant off until further notice by clicking on the Assistant, clicking Options, and then unticking the Use the Office Assistant box. When the Assistant is off, Excel will show a standard windows dialogue box when it requires information from you.

GETTING HELP WITHOUT THE OFFICE ASSISTANT

When you select <u>Microsoft Excel Help</u> from the <u>HELP</u> menu with the Office Assistant disabled (see page 84 for instructions), you will get a full-screen help display. The left-hand section of the screen allows you to access different help topics, while the right-hand section displays detailed information for you.

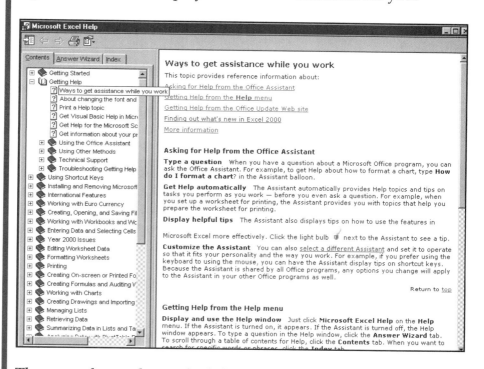

There are three tabs on the left side of the Microsoft Excel Help screen. The <u>Contents</u> tab lets you see the range of broad topics that Excel can help you with. Double-click on one to see a list of its sub-topics. You can select sub-topics until you have the information you need. The <u>Answer Wizard</u> tab will attempt to find an answer for a question that you type into it in natural English. Finally, the <u>Index</u> tab will find all help topics containing one or more words. Type the keywords into the box at the top, marked <u>1. Type Keywords</u>, or select one or more from the list marked <u>2. Or choose keywords</u>, then click <u>Search</u>. You can then choose a topic from the list marked <u>3. Choose a topic</u> to display in the right hand section of the screen.

SOME DESIGN TIPS

There are a few useful things to bear in mind when preparing an attractive, effective document for printing and distribution to others.

1. Don't use lots of different fonts – it looks messy and jumbled. Try to stick to two or three as a maximum.
2. Text formatting can be a very useful way of bringing attention to certain words, but only if it stands out by being uncommon. Use bold, italic and underline, but try not to overuse any of them if possible.
3. Think about the purpose that your document is to serve. If you are preparing data for a formal report, stick to a serious, serif font and do not add lots of colours, tints, shades and formatting.
4. A background tint to cells that hold important information – titles, totals and so on – can really make them stand out. Make sure the background doesn't overwhelm the text, though – just use a gentle tint.
5. Colour can be a great way of drawing attention, but like text formatting, that works best used sparingly. You can also use colour to categorize different types of cells.
6. A title centred across the page reads more like a headline. Sometimes this can be useful. Similarly, include page numbers for long documents.
7. Most of all though, make the work easy on the eye. If it is mind-bending or difficult to read, people will simply not bother, and all your work will be wasted.

SHOWING DATA

Getting your point across clearly involves making the best possible impact with your information. You want to be certain when that you are presenting data to another person, the items you wish to highlight are clearly demonstrated by the visual presentation of your work. In this section, we will look at some of the more advanced ways of displaying your information, including how to customize the appearance of your charts, how to create simple forms for printing, and how to create a pivot table.

6

ADVANCED CHARTS

The Chart Wizard is an extremely effective way of creating a visually attractive chart with the minimum of fuss. Sometimes however, you may want to go that little bit further. In this section, we'll look at different ways to make your charts a little more unique. As a bottom line, you can always select the chart and then re-start the chart wizard to modify any details you wish to revise.

MOVING AND RESIZING

You can change the position of the different elements of the chart diagram relative to one another within the boxed <u>Chart Area</u>. The chart itself, including its displayed data, axes, floor, walls, data table and axis labels, counts as one single object for these purposes, known as the <u>Plot Area</u>. The different titles you may or may not have (chart title, individual axis titles, and so on) each count as separate objects, and the legend box is also a separate item. You can click on the borders of each separate item, or select it from the drop-down list in the <u>Chart</u> toolbar – you will see that it is selected by the thick grey line around it – and increase its size with the scroll bars in the corners, or drag it around the <u>Chart Area</u> to move it. Note that the pieces within the <u>Plot Area</u> are all selectable, and if you click inside it, you may select a part of it, rather than the whole area.

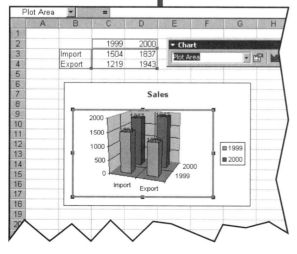

ADDING, MODIFYING AND REMOVING DATA

The easiest way to change the data for a chart is to modify it on the spreadsheet. Click on the chart, and the range of data that the chart is based on will be surrounded with a thin blue line, with series and point names surrounded in green and purple respectively. Change any data within the indicated range and lock the change by moving off the cell, and the chart will automatically update accordingly. This is shown in the two example pictures below.

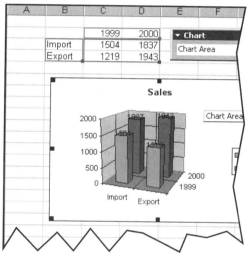

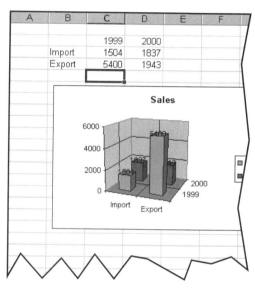

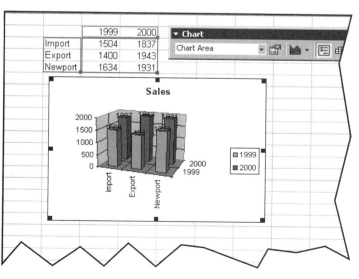

You can also add a new row of data just below your chart data range, or a new column just to the right of it, and then click and hold one of the scroll handles surrounding the chart data (the cursor will change to a thin black cross when it is ready to select a scroll handle), adjacent to your new data. Drag the blue line over your new row or column of data, and the chart will be updated to include the new data.

FORMATTING TEXT ELEMENTS

Each textual element within your chart can be formatted separately or collectively. To collectively modify all the text in the chart – which will apply the same text styles to all of it – double-click on the <u>Chart Area</u> background, outside of the <u>Plot Area</u> and the area of other elements. The best place to do this is generally towards the top left-hand corner. A dialog box entitled <u>Format Chart Area</u> will appear. If any other dialog arises, close it and try double-clicking slightly closer to the edge of the chart box.

Double-clicking on the <u>Chart Area</u> background will bring up the <u>Format Chart Area</u> box (right). Highlighting text and double-clicking on it will bring up the <u>Format Axis</u> box (below).

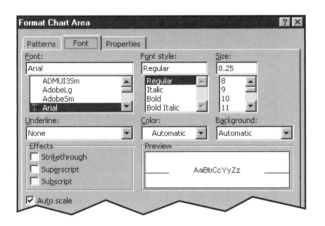

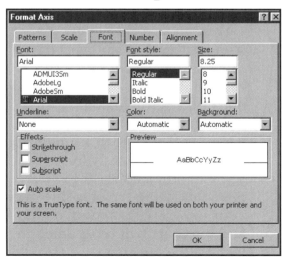

Select the <u>Font</u> tab on the above dialog box, and choose the options that you would like to apply, as usual. The preview will show you how the text is going to look. When you are happy with it, click <u>OK</u> and the text style will be applied to all the text on the chart. You can also format all the individual text elements in exactly the same way. Double-click exactly on the element itself, and a formatting options box for just that element will appear. If it has a text component, the <u>Format</u> dialog will have a <u>Font</u> tab. Click on that to access text formatting options, and then click <u>OK</u> to apply them.

FORMATTING DATA SERIES AND BACKGROUNDS

Changing the visual appearance of the different elements within the chart is as easy as changing the text formatting. Double-click on the element concerned, and if it has a graphical component, a <u>Patterns</u> tab will be visible within the <u>Format</u> dialogue. Click on this tab to get access to the visual formatting for that element – which can be as precise as an individual series of data.

The <u>Border</u>, <u>Area</u> and <u>Sample</u> boxes on this tab work in the way that we have already encountered. The <u>Fill Effects</u> box inside the <u>Area</u> section will show you the options you have for applying a textured fill. For some elements this will just be a standard pattern palette, but larger elements will be able to use a graded fill, a pre-set texture or even a picture from file. Click on an option to select it, and <u>OK</u> to apply it.

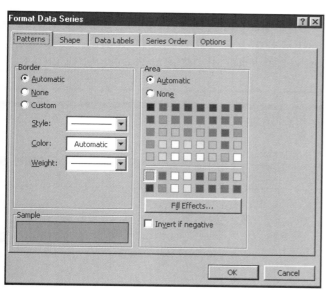

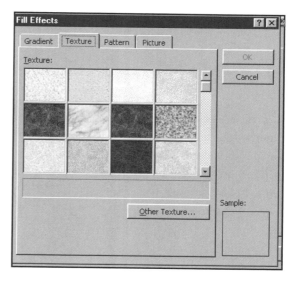

ADVANCED FORMATTING

There are many other advanced formatting tasks you can perform from the various elements' respective <u>Format</u> dialogues. Unfortunately, they are beyond the scope of this book, but full details are available within Excel's help system (see pages 84–85).

WORKING WITH FORMS

A form, like a template, is a fixed page (or pages) which can accept data in certain specific places so as to personalize the page, or to record or commemorate specific information within a set pattern. In other words, it's a type of document which you fill in the blanks on. This section will discuss how to create forms, and how to save them as template documents for future use. Note that Excel also uses the word Form to mean a fixed box for entering new data into when working with a database or large list – we'll discuss that type of form later on, in Chapter Nine.

WHEN TO USE A FORM

Whenever you are going to need to regularly produce documents that will look more or less the same but will involve new data, you should consider producing a form. In addition, if you require a paper form for people to fill in for some purpose – membership applications for a group, ballot papers, address slips, etc. – you should think about turning to Excel to help.

Forms are easy to generate using Excel. Expense Statements (right) and Invoices (next page) are just two useful examples.

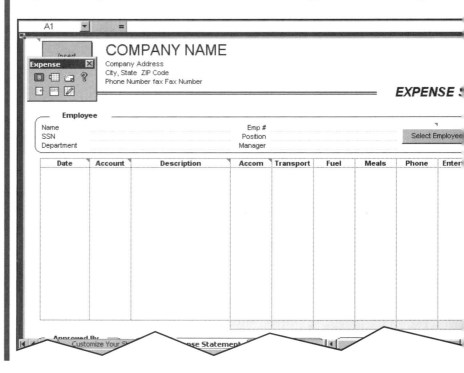

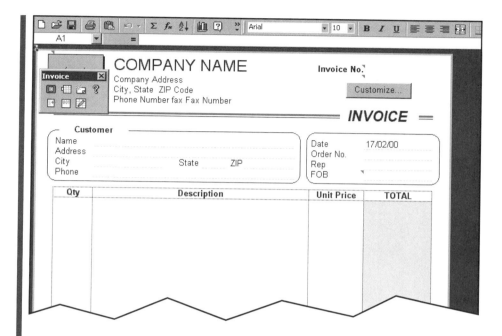

ARRANGING DATA

When you are creating a form, it is useful to start with an idea of how you want the finished item to look. Take some time to work out what items you want to include on the form, and how much space you think they should take up. Under default settings, a page on the printer will stretch across to approximately the end of Column I, and down to around Row 55, so that gives you an idea of how much space things will take up. Put in the pieces that are most important or that will take up the most space first; once they are in place, you can fit the less important elements around them.

Remember to use headings and cell borders to break the form up a bit. Group cells together to give you a large area for a heading or title, or apply patterns, shading or background images to make certain areas of the form stand out. If there are only a few places where you will be changing the information – as for an invoice – then unlock those cells you will need to change as discussed earlier, and then protect the sheet. With a bit of careful planning, you will find that it is easy to create an attractive form document.

THE IF FUNCTION

As we mentioned briefly earlier, functions are special programs built into Excel that let your cells perform simple calculations. This can be really useful when building a form – particularly the IF function, which lets a cell display one of two different entries depending on circumstances. To create an IF function, you need to specify what the test to perform is (the Condition), what to display if it passes (True), and what to display if it fails (False). The contents of the cell then look like this:

=IF(Condition, True, False)

To give you an example, let us consider a situation where you want to convert a decimal value on your form into an on-off switch of 1 or 0. If your decimal is less than 2.5, you want the switch indicator on your form to be off. Assuming that the decimal value is stored in cell B3 on your sheet, the appropriate IF statement, typed into the cell you want to display the result, would be:

=IF(B3<2.5,0,1)

In other words, IF is rather like the data version of conditional formatting – conditional contents, if you like. You can combine IF with all sorts of other functions to test more complicated situations, as we'll discuss later, in Chapter Seven.

One of the more significant ways of working with the IF statement to achieve impressive results is to use Switch Cells. The main limitation of IF is that you cannot use the full range of calculations and functions inside the True and False result parts of the statement. You can get around this though, by placing the functions and formulae you would like to use inside the IF decision within other cells, and then using the IF to decide which of them to activate. For example, your IF statement could read =IF(B3<2.5,K1,K2). K1 and K2 can hold as complicated a formula as you need, and the B3 value will switch the cell holding the IF statement from one to the other.

ADVANCED FORMS

If you know how to program Excel Macros (or Visual Basic), you can make use of the advanced form creation functions provided by the <u>Forms</u> toolbar. This sort of work is extremely powerful – you can have different selection and analysis tools built into the form, and even allow for it to be filled in on the web – but it is also very advanced, and is outside the scope of this book. The <u>Forms</u> toolbar can be displayed through the <u>Customize</u> option on the <u>TOOLS</u> menu, as discussed in Chapter Ten. Each of the elements provided on the toolbar can be incorporated quickly and easily into an Excel document, but then need to have effects programmed into it for full functionality.

The <u>Forms</u> toolbar. Call this up from the <u>TOOLS</u> menu.

USING FORMS LATER

Once you have a form finished and ready for use, the best thing to do is to save it as a template, as discussed in Chapter One. You also may like to unlock cells that you will want to be changeable, and then protect the worksheet, as discussed in Chapter Three.

TABLES

To the Excel user, "tables" can mean any one of a number of things. Later in this section you will discover PivotTables and further on through the book you will learn about one- and two-variable data-tables, but the most straightforward definition of a table is merely to refer to the information you have entered into your worksheet. Once you've created a table there are many things you can now do with it. Excel is a powerful tool which allows you format your data for output, manipulate the figures to extract the information you require and to "dig down" through the information to examine possibilities and options.

BUILDING A TABLE FOR PRINTING

The simplest thing you are going to want to do with your table is print it out. Even if you don't need the complex mathematical or financial functions available, Excel is still a great tool for entering, formatting and outputting data onto paper. Excel allows you to use standard formatting functions to create headings and subheadings and titles. In order to print a table effectively, you must define it as a print area. First, select the area you want to be printed, the click on Set Print Area from the Print Area item on the File menu. You should now notice a grid of dotted lines on your worksheet – these define the pages that will be printed out, as discussed in Chapter Five

USING CELL FORMULAS IN YOUR TABLE

Excel is good as a tool for laying out and displaying tables, but it comes into its own when you use cell formulas to link related cells together, enabling changes made in one cell to affect the contents of another (or more). Cell references – the names of cells, discussed earlier – can be used as variables in formulas. Cell Formulas fall into two categories – algebraic and function-based.

Algebraic formulas are simple to use, and based on standard mathematical symbols, such as "+" for adding or "/" for dividing. For instance, two numbers, in cells A1 and A2, could be added together by putting the formula "=A1+A2" in cell A3. Any changes to the numbers in cells A1 and A2 would be shown in the result in A3.

This image shows the calculation of the contents of cells A1 and A2 in cell A3. The formula is shown above the worksheet.

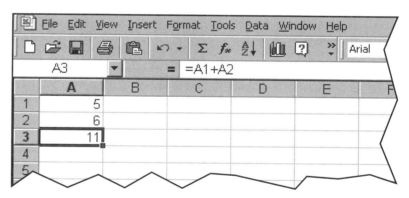

Function-based formulas use special keywords, recognised by Excel, to perform certain calculations on the data in cells. These range from simply adding two numbers together – the example above could be changed to use a function by altering the contents of A3 to read "=SUM(A1:A2)" – to the complex mathematical and statistical functions which are discussed elsewhere in this book.

REMINDER

Put an equals sign ("=") before any formula in a cell to let Excel know that it is to calculate it, and not to treat it as a text input.

WHAT IS A PIVOTTABLE?

A PivotTable is a powerful tool for interactively examining multiple fields of data in a simple and straightforward form. PivotTables allow you to move fields of a database from one axis to the other and immediately see the results. For instance, if you had a database showing the sales made by three salesmen of four different products each, when all three salesmen work in two different regions, and you have data across three months, you would imagine you'd need four, five or even six different charts to allow you to compare sales figures across the board. But with a PivotTable, you can have two or even three fields on one axis to compare the data by one category – say months – then shift the fields around again to compare different options, such as regional sales per salesman against product sold. It sounds complex, but a few examples and some experimentation will open up this powerful tool to you.

The data for a PivotTable can come from an existing Excel list (like the one shown below), database or PivotTable or from an external source. You can even use data from multiple worksheets to create your PivotTable, and Excel provides a simple and effective Wizard to help you.

1							
2	**Month**	**Region**	**Product**	**Sales**			
3	January	North	Sheep	3900			
4	January	South	Sheep	4500			
5	January	North	Cats	2800			
6	January	South	Cats	4300			
7	January	North	Dogs	4000			
8	January	South	Dogs	1000			
9	January	North	Things	3500			
10	January	South	Things	4900			
11	February	North	Sheep	8900			
12	February	South	Sheep	900			
13	February	North	Cats	200			
14	February	South	Cats	2700			
15	February	North	Dogs	9800			
16	February	South	Dogs	8300			
17	February	North	Things	4200			
18	February	South	Things	9500			
19	March	North	Sheep	0			
20	March	South	Sheep	8900			
21	March	North		2700			

THE PIVOTTABLE AND PIVOTCHART WIZARD

Select the <u>PivotTable and PivotChart Report</u> item from the <u>DATA</u> menu to start the <u>PivotTable Wizard</u>.

The first page of the Wizard allows to you to select the source of the data from which you want to create your PivotTable. If your data is in the form of an Excel list or database, make sure the worksheet holding your data is open, and select <u>Microsoft Excel list or database</u>. If your data is in an external database then select <u>External</u> data source. (We will look at using external data in more detail later in this book.) If you want to take information from two or more worksheets, select <u>Multiple consolidation ranges</u> and if you already have a PivotTable on which you wish to base your new PivotTable, select <u>Another PivotTable or PivotChart</u>. Click on <u>Next</u>.

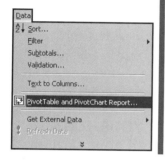

On the second page of the Wizard, you select the location of the data you'll be using for your PivotTable. In this and the next section, we'll be assuming you're using a database in your current worksheet, so juct click <u>Next</u>. The third page of the PivotTable Wizard enables you place your PivotTable in a new or existing worksheet.

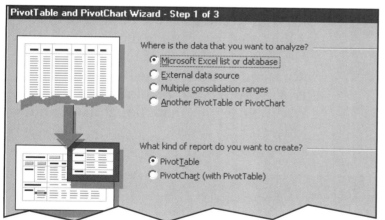

Using the <u>PivotTable and PivotChart Wizard</u> is simple, just follow the instructions.

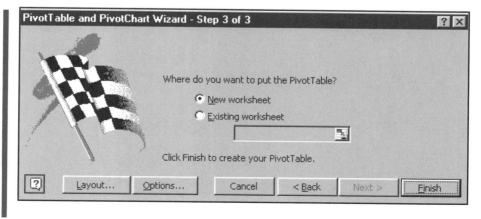

Once the PivotTable has been placed, you have to choose which fields go where. On the PivotTable dialog box, a list of your data series is available to be dragged into either the rows or columns of your new table. You can drag the series to place as you see fit, depending on what items you want to compare. Page items allow for an entirely new page for each part of that category. Row elements display their subdivisions vertically; columns do so horizontally. Data items are the series that is displayed in the body of the table.

TYPE & LOCATION OF YOUR DATA

PivotTables work best with numerical data, although they can be used for statistical purposes to calculate the occurence of various pieces of data in a table. A simple cross-referenced table of two sets of information is too simple to require a PivotTable. The most suitable data for a PivotTable is information that has a number of hierarchical levels.

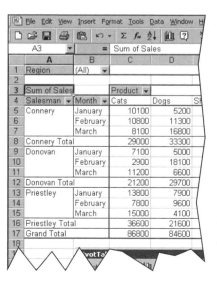

Fill in the blank table by dragging data series – i.e. categories – onto the row, column, page and date areas.

Data for a PivotTable can be placed anywhere in a worksheet and the PivotTable can be placed on that same worksheet, or on another sheet in the same book.

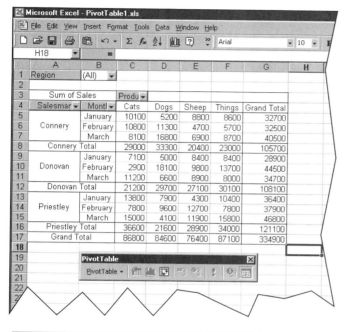

PIVOTING THE PIVOTTABLE

Once you have the PivotTable completed, you can now use its abilities to look at your data from different viewpoints. The most obvious feature of a PivotTable is the ability to drag the fields from one axis to another:

This enables you to see the data in different relationships. You can also drag fields to the Page Corner, and select individual pages.

You can get different totals to compare figures by dragging different data series to different positions.

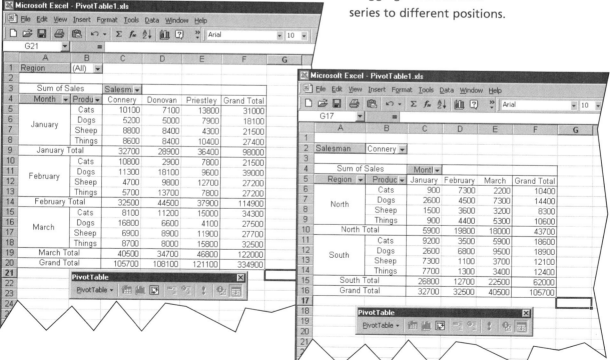

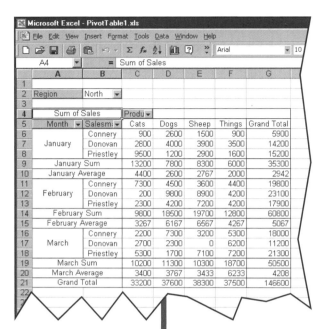

SUBTOTALS AND GRAND TOTALS

With a PivotTable, you can request further information for each field. By double-clicking on a field button, you can select subtotals and totals, averages, counts, deviations and other analytical functions to be displayed.

Using the PivotTable Field dialog box, you can also alter the location of the field between Row, Column and Page – which is similar to interactively dragging it across a PivotTable – and alter the Subtotals and Grand Totals that are displayed, and in the detail they show.

You can change settings to display averages and other values as well as – or instead of – totals.

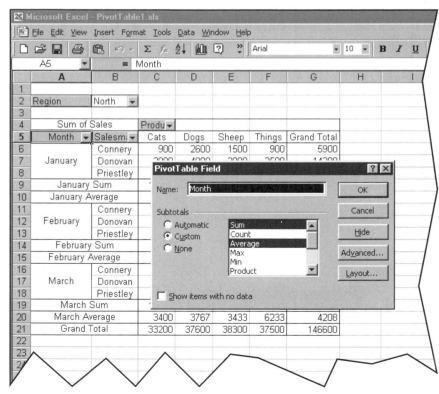

ADDING MORE

7

In this chapter, we'll look at the basics of creating simple images with the aid of Excel's built in drawing tools, bringing pictures, clip-art and other more complicated graphics into a spreadsheet, and importing and exporting text – all of which will go a long way to helping you make your worksheets more attractive and effective.

In addition, we'll have a look at the range of different built-in functions available to make your worksheets more powerful.

DRAWING OBJECTS

Excel has a class of image types that are referred to as Drawing Objects. These are, literally, objects that are drawings. They include AutoShapes, WordArt and line art, and they are a swift and powerful way of adding simple, custom-made illustrations to a worksheet. In this section, we'll look at using drawing objects and getting the most from them.

THE DRAWING TOOLBAR

The most effective way to get access to the various drawing objects and their related functions is by activating the Drawing Toolbar. You can do this by clicking on the <u>Drawing</u> Toolbar icon on the Standard Toolbar – which will cause the toolbar to appear at the bottom of the Excel window. The <u>Drawing</u> icon looks like this:

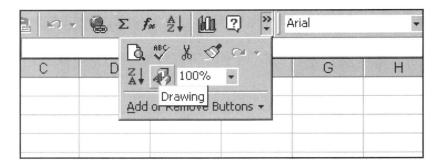

Access the Drawing toolbar by using the icon, found in the standard toolbar.

LINE ART

The most basic method of drawing using Excel is to join several pieces of line art, that is, to use the most basic of all possible drawing tools – a rectangle, an oval, a straight line, and an arrow. You can do quite a lot more with these basic items than you may think, such as organization charts, frames, simple geometric constructs, and more. Pieces of line art, like all drawing objects, are not automatically fixed to the cell structure of the sheet, so you can start a rectangle in the middle of a cell as easily as at its edge.

Access the line art tools by clicking on the relevant icons in the toolbar and drawing your shape on your worksheet.

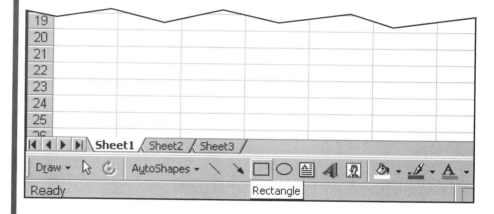

To use a line art tool, click on it to select it, then click at the start point in your worksheet, and drag until your line art is the right size. Sometimes, you will want to constrain the piece. Constraining means to make sure that lines run parallel to the grid (for <u>Lines</u> and <u>Arrows</u>) or make geometrically 'perfect' shapes – squares for the <u>Rectangle</u> tool, and circles for the <u>Oval</u>. To constrain line art – and <u>AutoShapes</u> – click on the <u>Shift</u> key and hold it down from before you start drawing until after you finish.

ART AND SHAPES

Excel thinks of the Line Art tools as simple AutoShapes, so they obey all the rules for AutoShapes that you'll find over the page.

AUTOSHAPES
In addition to the simple elements discussed on the previous page, Excel also provides you with a wide range of other shapes to help make it easier for you to produce the visual effects that you require. Click on the <u>AutoShapes</u> button on the <u>Drawing</u> toolbar, and you'll see a list of optional categories. If there is a down-arrow at the bottom of the menu indicating more options, leave the mouse over the menu for a few seconds to reveal the less commonly-used categories.

When you've found an AutoShape you'd like to add in, click on it, then just click and drag, as on the previous page, to insert your shape into the worksheet.

1 Click on <u>AutoShapes</u> (above) and choose the shape(s) you wish to use from the many dropdown menus (examples below).

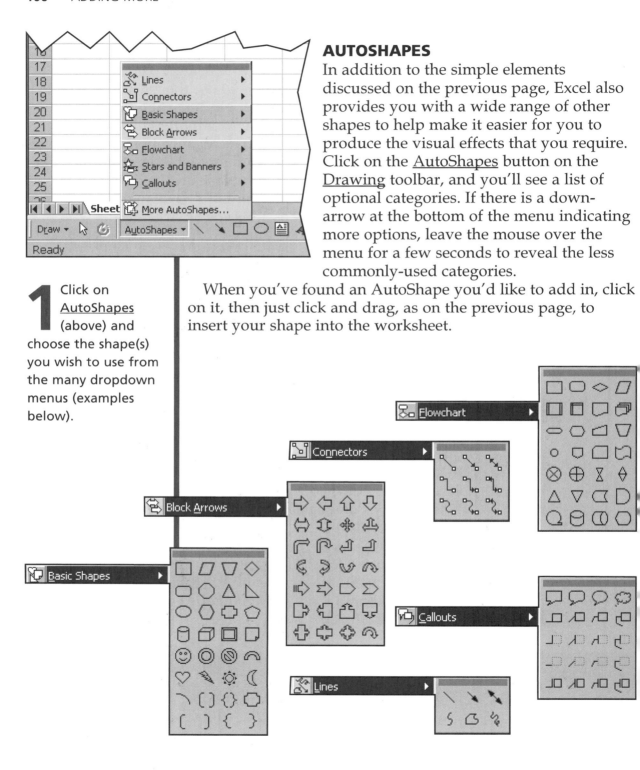

WORDART

The WordArt program – which is in fact a standard addition to Excel, and not an actual part of it – gives you a quick and simple way to make text look interesting.

1 Click on the Insert WordArt button on the Drawing tool bar.

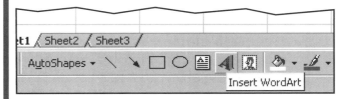

2 The WordArt Gallery will appear. Click on a style of WordArt you like.

3 Type your text into the Edit WordArt Text box and click OK. Your new WordArt will be placed on the sheet. You can click and drag it to move it around as you require.

TEXT BOXES

You can also create a box of plain text as a drawing object. Click on the Text Box icon and then click and drag on the sheet to create a text box. You can then move and format that text as you would any other drawing object.

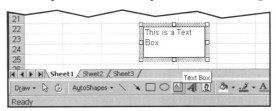

A text box, created using the Text Box icon.

POSITIONING DRAWING OBJECTS

To select any drawing object, click on an opaque portion of it – in other words, a piece that obscures the cell lines behind it. It will become selected, with scroll handles at the corners and edges, and a grey box around it if it holds (or can hold) text. You can enlarge the object by clicking on a scroll handle and dragging it, or move it by clicking on the item itself and dragging it around. Holding <u>Shift</u> down while you do this will constrain the object to a ratio of its current shape. To select a second object simultaneously, hold <u>Shift</u> down while clicking on the next object. The scroll handles will be visible around both objects. Once you have more than one object selected, you can set them to move around as one item – known as a group, the equivalent of Merged cells – by clicking on the <u>Draw</u> menu on the <u>Drawing</u> toolbar, and selecting the option <u>Group</u>, which you can undo again with the option <u>Ungroup</u>. If you can't see it, move your mouse over the down-arrows at the bottom of the menu to expand the menu up.

Grouping two or more shapes together will mean that they are treated as one item.

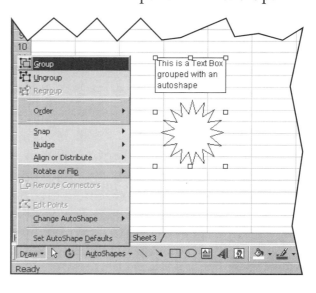

You can also make an object go behind or come in front of another using the <u>Order</u> sub-menu of the <u>Draw</u> menu, align it to the cell grid from the <u>Snap</u> submenu, or rotate or invert it from the <u>Rotate or Flip</u> menu.

FORMATTING DRAWING OBJECTS

All drawing objects can be formatted in exactly the same way, which is similar to the way that chart elements can be formatted – place your mouse over the object that you wish to format, and double-click on it. That object's particular Formatting dialog box will be displayed (or the Edit Text box for WordArt, whose Formatting dialog can be accessed by right-clicking on the piece and selecting the Format WordArt option). These dialogs differ only in the options they allow – an Autoshape which does not include a built-in text box (the Callouts have one, as they are speech bubbles) will not have a text format bar, for example. The most useful tabs of the dialog box are going to be the Colors and Lines tab…

… and the Font and Alignment tabs if the object does (or can) contain text.

These behave in exactly the same way as the formatting tabs that we have already encountered. Most AutoShapes can display textures as well as patterns, so to access those remember to click on the Color bar of the Colors and Lines tab, and then on the Fill Effects box, and explore the various tabs of the Fill Effects dialog that appears.

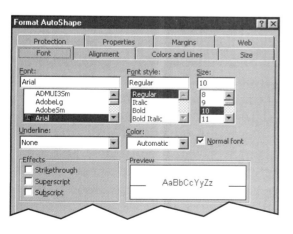

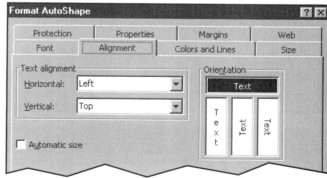

Adjust all aspects of the text in your Autoshapes by using the Format AutoShape dialog box, and its associated tabs.

IMPORTING AND EXPORTING

There are many ways to include data from external files into your Excel worksheet, and indeed to save the information stored inside it for use by other programs themselves. In this section, we'll have a look at some of the different ways to work with other types of data from inside Excel.

Some examples of Excel documents saved as space, comma and tab delimited.

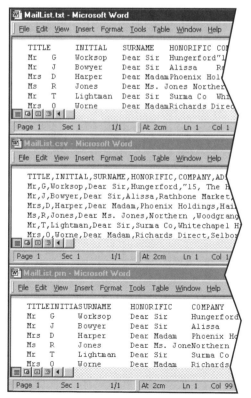

SIMPLE EXPORTS

The easiest way of getting your data out of Excel in a form that can be read easily by many other applications is to save your worksheet as plain text. In this format, only the currently active worksheet will be saved, and all graphics, formatting and other special features will be lost. Where you have equations, only the result of that equation, as displayed on the screen, will be saved. Despite these limitations, it can be a very useful function. Click on Save As... from the FILE menu, and then click on the Save As Type... box. A long drop-down list of save types will appear. The three main plain text options are called Text (Tab Delimited) (*.txt), CSV (Comma Delimited) (*.csv), and Formatted Text (Space Delimited) (*.prn). These options change the way that Excel marks the end of a cell boundary within your new text file – the 'delimiting' character specified is used. Tab delimited and comma delimited are likely to be the most useful options.

OLDER WORKSHEETS

There are a wide range of older program files that Excel 2000 can understand. As well as being able to decipher saved workbooks from all the previous versions of Excel down to and including version 4.0, it can also understand web pages, text files, Web Query files, Macro files, Data Interchange files and spreadsheets created by Lotus, Quattro Pro, MS Works and dBase. To open an older file, select <u>Open</u> from the <u>FILE</u> menu, and navigate to the file as you would if it were a standard Excel file. With some formats the conversion process will mean that some formatting and other advanced data gets lost, but the core information will be translated.

Excel can intelligently open files from many other formats, shown in the popup list.

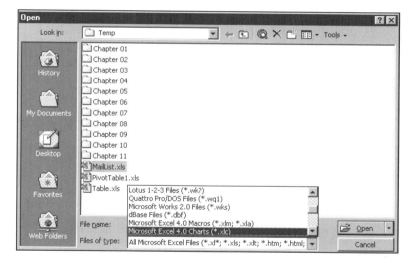

Saving files in a format compatible with older programs is just as easy. From the <u>Save As...</u> dialog off the <u>FILE</u> menu, click on the <u>Save As Type...</u>. box, then scroll down the list until you find a type of file that is sufficient for your needs. For colleagues with older versions of Excel on the PC, the best file type is generally the one called <u>Microsoft Excel 97–2000 & 5.0/95 Workbook</u> – quite a mouthful, but it is an extremely versatile format. For colleagues who will want to use your file on a Macintosh computer, the best file type to select is the one called <u>Microsoft Excel 5.0/95 Workbook</u>, which is compatible with recent versions of Excel for the Mac.

IMPORTING PICTURES

You can add a picture from your own computer's files into an Excel worksheet without any difficulty.

1 From the INSERT menu, select the Picture submenu, and click on From File....

2 Browse through the Insert Picture dialog box to the location of your picture.

3 Click on the picture you would like to insert, when you have found it.

4 Click OK. The picture you have selected will now be inserted as a drawing object, and can be resized, moved and formatted like other drawing objects.

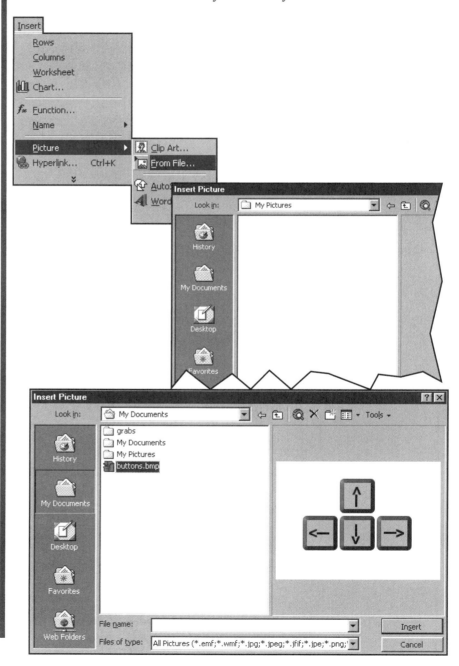

IMPORTING CLIPART

Importing a piece of ClipArt is similar to importing a picture from file, and it can be similarly modified afterwards.

1 Click on the ClipArt icon ... or select from the INSERT menu.

2 The Insert ClipArt dialog will be displayed. A list of ClipArt categories you have installed will be shown. Note that ClipArt will only be available if you installed it with the rest of Excel.

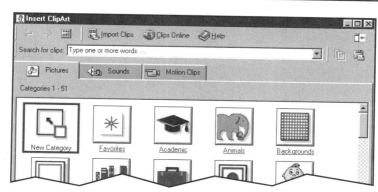

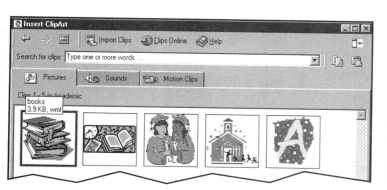

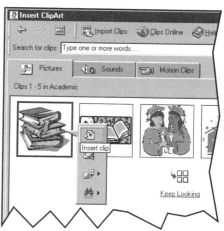

3 Double-click on a category of ClipArt, and after a moment a list of available ClipArt files in that category will be displayed. Find a piece that fits your needs, and click on it.

4 A small speech-bubble shaped dialog will appear. Click on Insert Clip and your new Clip Art will be inserted into your document.

INSERTING OBJECTS

In addition to including an image inside an Excel spreadsheet as simply a visual addition, it is possible to add in an image that you can edit and manipulate while inside Excel through the program that created it. In other words, you can add in a Microsoft Word letter and call Word open to modify it, or add in a PhotoShop image and call PhotoShop open to edit it, and so on. This type of inclusion is called an Object, a term which specifically denotes a link to another application.

1 Select <u>Object...</u> from the <u>INSERT</u> menu.

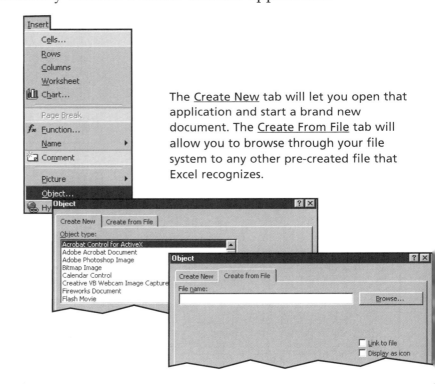

The <u>Create New</u> tab will let you open that application and start a brand new document. The <u>Create From File</u> tab will allow you to browse through your file system to any other pre-created file that Excel recognizes.

2 The <u>Object</u> dialog box will appear. Select one of the options (see right), and click <u>OK</u>.

3 The new Object will be inserted into your worksheet. You can re-size it or move it as you would a drawing object. Double-click on it to open it in the application that created it.

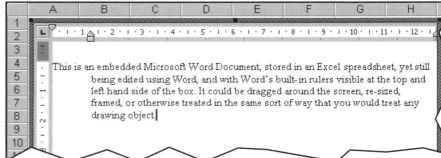

This is an embedded Microsoft Word Document, stored in an Excel spreadsheet, yet still being edited using Word, and with Word's built-in rulers visible at the top and left hand side of the box. It could be dragged around the screen, re-sized, framed, or otherwise treated in the same sort of way that you would treat any drawing object.

OBJECT LINKING AND EMBEDDING

Inserting an object makes use of a Microsoft Windows internal function called OLE, or Object Linking and Embedding. This is a clever piece of programming that allows you to do what was discussed on the previous page – to link files between documents on different applications, for easier cross-editing and for automatic updating. What is more interesting for our purposes is the way that OLE allows the Clipboard to cross-reference files. In short, you can load a document, image, spreadsheet or other file into an OLE application, select it and, from the application's Edit menu, choose <u>Copy</u>. You can then switch to any other OLE application, make sure the file you want to place the previous item into is active, and choose <u>Paste</u> from the <u>Edit</u> menu. The object will be pasted in exactly as it was in the previous application (although sometimes it will be shown on the screen as the application's icon). The uses of this facility start at the lower end with things like pasting an Excel chart into a Word document or a PowerPoint presentation, and get more sophisticated from there.

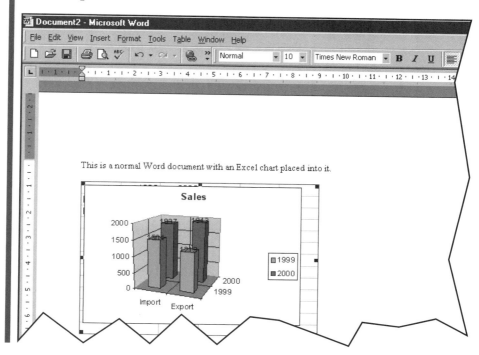

This Word document has had a chart that was generated in Excel placed in it.

AN INTRODUCTION TO FUNCTIONS

As we've seen in other places, a function is a special piece of programming code that you can access in a pre-defined way to allow a cell to perform calculations on data, or to analyse other elements of the computer environment that Excel is running in, such as today's date. Functions are one of the most powerful aspects of Excel, and can allow you to achieve a lot of complex results. In this section we'll give you an introduction to functions, and then let you know what the functions at your disposal are.

WHAT A FUNCTION LOOKS LIKE

Every function has a pre-defined name that you can use within a cell formula in place of a cell reference. The function's name is always followed by a pair of brackets and is usually written in capitals, so that they look like this:

FUNCTIONNAME()

Different functions have different requirements for what goes inside the brackets – some functions, that do not need to refer to any other data, keep the brackets empty as above, while others may take one or more cell references or other items of data. Bits of information put inside the brackets (known as Variables) are passed to the function, and it must be in the right order for the function to work correctly. Although this sounds complicated, all you have to do is check which variables a particular function needs, and make sure that you enter them in the right order – check Excel's Help system with the name of the function you want to use for specific instructions. For a detailed look at passing variables to a function, and dealing with logical syntax, see Chapter Eleven.

DATE AND TIME FUNCTIONS

The functions related to date and time all deal, unsurprisingly, with the date and/or time. Most of them give information regarding "now", but others can give you information on where a certain day falls within a year, how many days away from now a date is, how many working days there are between two dates, and so on. The Date and time functions are:

DATE()	MINUTE()	TODAY()
DATEVALUE()	MONTH()	WEEKDAY()
DAY()	NETWORKDAYS()	WORKDAY()
DAYS360()	NOW()	YEAR()
EDATE()	SECOND()	YEARFRAC()
EOMONTH()	TIME()	
HOUR()	TIMEVALUE()	

TEXT FUNCTIONS

There are a number of functions that allow you to manipulate textual information. A piece of textual data is known as a String, and strings can include numbers and symbols as necessary. Text functions let you work with strings, including looking at individual letters within a string, joining strings together, and converting numbers or dates into text.
The Text Functions are:

CHAR()	LEFT()	SEARCH()
CLEAN()	LEN()	SUBSTITUTE()
CODE()	LOWER()	T()
CONCATENATE()	MID()	TEXT()
DOLLAR()	PROPER()	TRIM()
EXACT()	REPLACE()	UPPER()
FIND()	REPT()	VALUE()
FIXED()	RIGHT()	

LOGICAL AND INFORMATIONAL FUNCTIONS

Excel provides a number of useful facilities for testing logical conditions – that is, whether something is true or false, and so on – and also for gathering information, looking up cells and examining databases. One particular set of Information functions, known as the IS Functions (because they all start with IS) will be discussed in greater detail in Chapter Eleven.

The Logical, Information, Lookup and Database functions are:

AND()	ISODD()	ROW()
FALSE()	ISREF()	ROWS()
IF()	ISTEXT()	TRANSPOSE()
NOT()	N()	VLOOKUP()
OR()	NA()	DAVERAGE()
TRUE()	TYPE()	DCOUNT()
CELL()	ADDRESS()	DCOUNTA()
COUNTBLANK()	AREAS()	DGET()
ERROR.TYPE()	CHOOSE()	DMAX()
INFO()	COLUMN()	DMIN()
ISBLANK()	COLUMNS()	DPRODUCT()
ISERR()	HLOOKUP()	DSTDEV()
ISERROR()	HYPERLINK()	DSTDEVP()
ISEVEN()	INDEX()	DSUM()
ISLOGICAL()	INDIRECT()	DVAR()
ISNA()	LOOKUP()	DVARP()
ISNONTEXT()	MATCH()	GETPIVOTDATA()
ISNUMBER()	OFFSET()	

MATHEMATICAL AND FINANCIAL FUNCTIONS

Traditionally, spreadsheet programs such as Excel were used mostly for financial analysis. Things are no longer quite so simple, but Excel retains a wide range of different functions for working with numbers. In addition to the ones listed here, the Analysis ToolPak – which, like the ClipArt gallery, is actually a separate program to Excel but comes with the MS Office – contains a number of engineering functions for manipulating values.

The Math, Statistical and Financial functions are as follows:

ABS()	COSH()	FACT()
ACCRINT()	COUNT()	FACTDOUBLE()
ACCRINTM()	COUNTA()	FDIST()
ACOS()	COUNTIF()	FINV()
ACOSH()	COUPDAYBS()	FISHER()
AMORDEGRC()	COUPDAYS()	FISHERINV()
AMORLINC()	COUPDAYSNC()	FLOOR()
ASIN()	COUPNCD()	FORECAST()
ASINH()	COUPNUM()	FREQUENCY()
ATAN()	COUPPCD()	FTEST()
ATAN2()	COVAR()	FV()
ATANH()	CRITBINOM()	FVSCHEDULE()
AVEDEV()	CUMIPMT()	GAMMADIST()
AVERAGE()	CUMPRINC()	GAMMAINV()
AVERAGEA()	DB()	GAMMALN()
BETADIST()	DDB()	GCD()
BETAINV()	DEGREES()	GEOMEAN()
BINOMDIST()	DEVSQ()	GROWTH()
CEILING()	DISC()	HARMEAN()
CHIDIST()	DOLLARDE()	HYPGEOMDIST()
CHIINV()	DOLLARFR()	INT()
CHITEST()	DURATION()	INTERCEPT()
COMBIN()	EFFECT()	INTRATE()
CONFIDENCE()	EVEN()	IPMT()
CORREL()	EXP()	IRR()
COS()	EXPONDIST()	KURT()

LARGE()	PERCENTRANK()	STDEVA()
LCM()	PERMUT()	STDEVP()
LINEST()	PI()	STDEVPA()
LN()	PMT()	STEYX()
LOG()	POISSON()	SUBTOTAL()
LOG10()	POWER()	SUM()
LOGEST()	PPMT()	SUMIF()
LOGINV()	PRICE()	SUMPRODUCT()
LOGNORMDIST()	PRICEDISC()	SUMSQ()
MAX()	PRICEMAT()	SUMX2MY2()
MAXA()	PROB()	SUMX2PY2()
MDETERM()	PRODUCT()	SUMXMY2()
MDURATION()	PV()	SYD()
MEDIAN()	QUARTILE()	TAN()
MIN()	QUOTIENT()	TANH()
MINA()	RADIANS()	TBILLEQ()
MINVERSE()	RAND()	TBILLPRICE()
MIRR()	RANDBETWEEN()	TBILLYIELD()
MMULT()	RANK()	TDIST()
MOD()	RATE()	TINV()
MODE()	RECEIVED()	TREND()
MROUND()	ROMAN()	TRIMMEAN()
MULTINOMIAL()	ROUND()	TRUNC()
NEGBINOMDIST()	ROUNDDOWN()	TTEST()
NOMINAL()	ROUNDUP()	VAR()
NORMDIST()	RSQ()	VARA()
NORMINV()	SERIESSUM()	VARP()
NORMSDIST()	SIGN()	VARPA()
NORMSINV()	SIN()	VDB()
NPER()	SINH()	WEIBULL()
NPV()	SKEW()	XIRR()
ODD()	SLN()	XNPV()
ODDFPRICE()	SLOPE()	YIELD()
ODDFYIELD()	SMALL()	YIELDDISC()
ODDLPRICE()	SQRT()	YIELDMAT()
ODDLYIELD()	SQRTPI()	ZTEST()
PEARSON()	STANDARDIZE()	
PERCENTILE()	STDEV()	

DATA ANALYSIS

Excel provides several useful ways of analysing your data both mathematically and graphically. In this section, we'll look at two different methodologies of data analysis – with a data map on the one hand, and with mathematical and statistical analysis and goal-solving tools on the other.

DATA MAPS

Mapping geographical data used to be an extremely expensive and laborious process that required complex, specialised software and, sometimes, skilled consultants. Excel can now provide this facility in a simple, convenient way through the Microsoft Map program, an optional component of the Microsoft Office.

USING A GEOGRAPHICAL DATA MAP

Data Maps are an extremely effective way of displaying information that is linked or tied to geographical locations. Regional sales figures are a good example of this sort of material, especially when different reps are involved with overlapping areas. Product penetration, market research and customer sites are also all excellent examples of cases where a data map can be useful.

LOOKING FOR A MAP

If you cannot find Microsoft Map on your system (it's normally listed as an object type within the Insert Object dialog), you may need to install it separately. If this is the case, re-run the Microsoft Office Setup program and select Microsoft Map for installation.

PREPARING YOUR DATA FOR MAPPING

Getting your data ready to map is not difficult, but there is a particular format that you need to make use of. You need to have your data in one continuous table, with the left-most column holding the geographical information. This information needs to be in the form of standard country names or abbreviations, county/state full names or 2-digit UK postcode or / 5-digit US zipcode. Additionally, it is worth adding a header bar to the data columns, to make it easier to format the map when the time comes.

This chart features text and numerical information, both of which will be used in your map.

	A	B	C	D	E	F
1	Sales	Waters	Price			
2	Hampshire	450	324			
3	Berkshire	630	295			
4	Wiltshire	325	540			
5	Oxfordshire	533	422			

CREATING A DATA MAP
Once you have your data complete and in place, creating a basic data map is simple.

1 Select your data range, making sure that your geographical information column is the leftmost column of your range, and that the location names are spelt correctly.

2 From the INSERT menu, select Object... and the Insert Object dialog will appear. From the Create New tab, scroll down the list titled Object Type until you find Microsoft Map. Click on that and select OK.

3 A new map will be created, based on your data as appropriate.

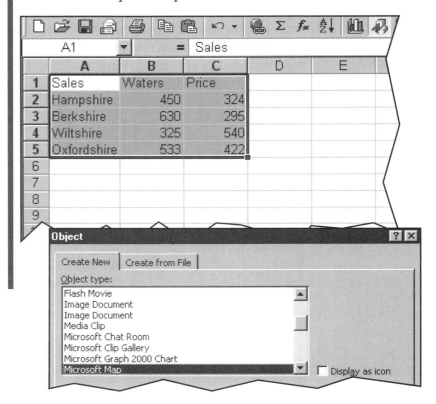

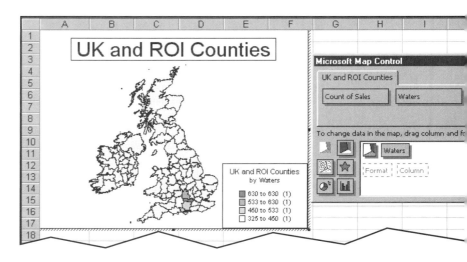

MAP MATCHING AND MANUAL SELECTION

In some circumstances, where Map is uncertain as to the geographical range you require, you will be asked to select the correct map from a dialogue entitled Multiple Maps Available. In other cases, the program may not recognize the regions you have specified at all, and may present you with a list of maps that it can understand – in this instance, make a note of the nearest map to your needs, press Esc to exit the creation program, and then Delete to get rid of the blank box created by the insertion process. Check your spelling, and that the geographical areas you want to map make sense to the nearest map available to what you want, then try again.

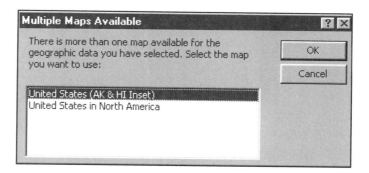

Alternatively, select the map that offers regions closest to the ones you need, and click OK. Then, from the Tools menu, select the Labeller option. The Map Labels dialog will appear. Click on the drop-down menu and, if there are multiple options, select the one that seems most likely to include the regional names you need (e.g. World Countries and Regions, rather than World Oceans), and click OK, then hold the mouse over the regions you wish to refer to, and their correct name will be displayed in a yellow box. Note down the correct names of the areas you want to map, then proceed as above, pressing Esc and Delete, revising your data, and starting again.

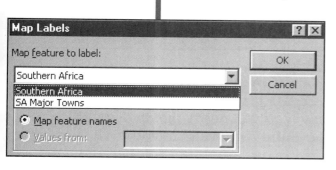

THE MAP CONTROL TOOLBAR

When you double-click on a Microsoft Map object to activate editing it, Excel hands control of the menus and toolbars over to the Map program. Excel's normal functions are superseded until you click on a cell outside the area of the map or press Escape. The following menus and toolbar functions are available from within Microsoft Map:

A map embedded in an Excel document. Use the Map tools (below the menu bar) to adjust it.

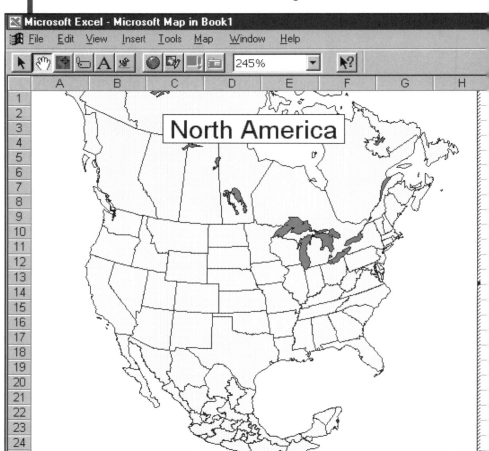

ZOOMING AND CENTRING THE MAP

Once you have your data keyed through to the correct geographic mapping, you will notice that by default Microsoft Map shows you the entire regional map you have selected. If your data is clustered in one area – say Southern England for example, which you would use the UK and ROI Counties map to examine – you will want to concentrate on that area. The first step is to pick the centre of your map:

1 From the <u>Map</u> toolbar, select the <u>Center Map</u> icon.

2 Click on a position close to the center of your data. The map will immediately move to put the location you just clicked on at the center of your map.

3 You can also click and drag the map around manually – select the <u>Grabber</u>, then click and drag to fine-position the map.

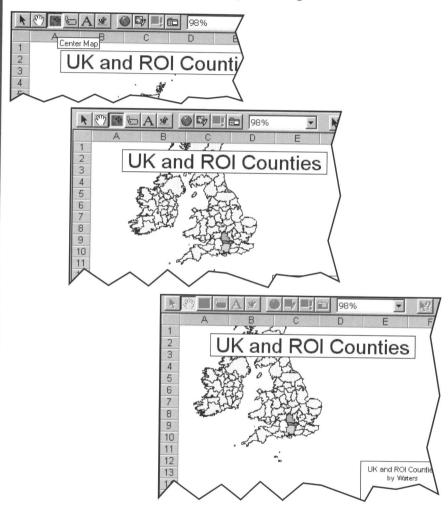

Once the map is centred to your satisfaction, you can zoom in on your region with the <u>Zoom Percentage of Map</u> dropdown button. It is generally best to increase the percentage to as high a level as possible while still showing all of your data is visible on the screen. In addition to selecting a pre-set value, you can also add a custom Zoom value of your choice in from 50% to 1,000,000%

DEPICTING VALUES

Data can be displayed in a number of different ways within your map. There are six different data display tools that can be used, called <u>Value Shading</u>, <u>Category Shading</u>, <u>Dot Density</u>, <u>Graduated Symbol</u>, <u>Column Chart</u> and <u>Pie Chart</u>. Each option can be used no more than once on any given Map. To use a display tool, go to the <u>Map</u> Control box and drag the appropriate tool icon from the palette on the left onto the grey "format" button in the white area, and then drag a data series from the list at the top down next to it onto the grey "column" button. The map will be updated with the new information. If another grey column button appears next to your data, you can add a subsequent data series into that display – as in with a Pie Chart, which will display the percentage of the total for that region that each different data series makes up. If no additional button appears, that display method can display just one data series at at time. However, you can have several different display styles active at one time, so that you could display reps' regions by colour and their sales in an individual area by scatter dots. Note that only the two chart types are capable of displaying more than one data series. Because of this, if your data has several series to be considered cumulatively, it is worth creating a Totals series as the last column of your data.

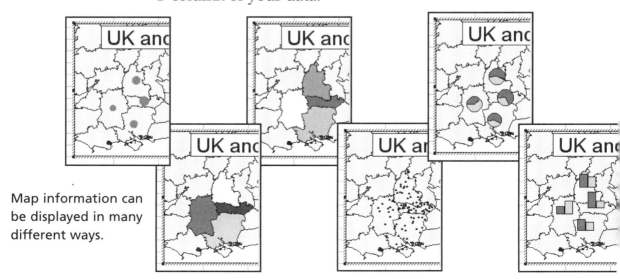

Map information can be displayed in many different ways.

FEATURES AND LABELS

Microsoft Map is aware of several different features that can be added to a map, such as major roads and rivers, cities, airports, regional names and so on. These features can be displayed on your map by clicking on the Features option from the Map menu, and selecting the features in the Map Features box that you want to include from the list available for that map, then clicking OK.

You can also add a textual label for either data values or map feature names by clicking the Map Labels icon, selecting either Map Features or a data range from the drop-down pick list, and then running the mouse pointer over the map. The pointer will drag a label box with it, which continually updates to show you the correct current label. Left-click to place that label at the current cursor position.

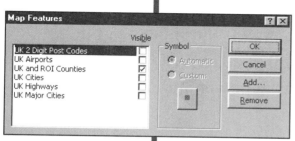

Use the Map Features (above) and Map Labels (right) dialog boxes to add to your maps.

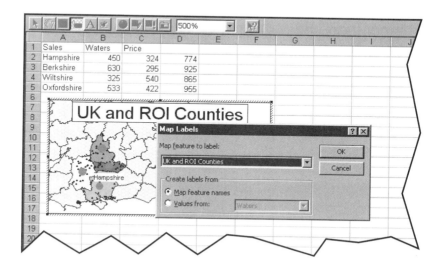

A QUICK NOTE ON FORMATTING

As you would expect, each element added to the basic map can be formatted to a greater or lesser extent. There is no room to go into details, but double-clicking on an object will bring up the appropriate format dialogue.

DATA ANALYSIS AND STATISTICS

Excel contains some highly complex and exceedingly powerful functions for analysing data in a worksheet. Most are highly specialized and come under a "if you don't know what they are, you don't need them" umbrella, but we will look at most of them here to give you an idea of the power and capabilities available to you.

DATA TABLES FOR WHAT-IF?

Data tables allow you to apply an equation to one or two lists of data values (often a series). This could be used, for instance, for a simple "What-If?" simulation, applying a "profit-per-customer" equation to a series of potential customer figures to see how many customers would be required to break-even in a new venture. To set up a one-variable table, enter the equation that you want to solve into the first cell of a row (the Equation Cell – an example is shown below). The numeric value for this equation to calculate should be a cell reference to a cell that must be – and stay – empty (the Input Cell), that Excel will use as temporary storage for your series of data. Then enter a series of values that you want Excel to enter into your equation, starting in the cell one column right and one row above the cell holding the formula (the Data Cells).

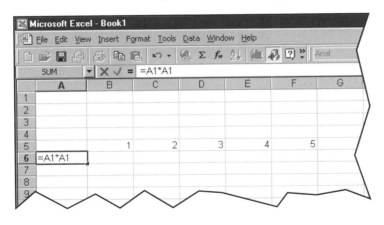

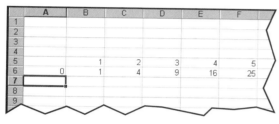

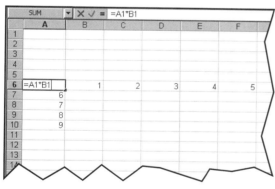

Then select the range of cells containing the Equation Cells and the Data Cells and click on the <u>Table</u> option on the <u>DATA</u> menu (left).

Enter the cell reference for the Input Cell (**not** the Equation Cell) into the <u>Row Input Cell</u> text entry box and click <u>OK</u>. The cells directly below each data value in the Data Cells will be filled with the result of plugging that data value into your equation (shown left).

A two-variable table is set up in a similar way, but a column of data values is entered directly below the Equation Cell, the row of data is entered on the same line as the Equation Cell and not the one above, and two blank input cells are required. Now the equation can refer to input cells for both the row and the column, and a grid of possible values is produced showing all permutations of row and column inputs (left).

EDITING TABLES

Tables are a real-time function – if you change a data value in either the input row or column, you will immediately see changes to the results in the grid. If you want to edit the values given as results, you first need to convert the results to standard values – at the moment they are calculated figures and cannot be edited.

Select the table and the click <u>Copy</u> on the <u>Edit</u> menu. If you do not need the table any more, you can copy the values straight back over the table – otherwise select a new location on the worksheet to put the values. Select <u>Paste Special</u> from the <u>Edit</u> menu (shown left) and choose the <u>Values</u> radio button in the <u>Paste</u> group. Click <u>OK</u> and a copy of the table will be pasted which contains values that you can edit.

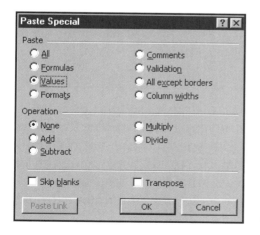

SCENARIOS

Scenarios are sets of different values that refer to a cell or cells you have chosen from specific locations in your worksheet. You can then use these changing cells as part of calculations, predictions, charts or other figures, and at a later date swap the scenario sets around without disturbing the rest of your work. Thus you could save a number of different versions of figures ("Year One", "Year Two", etc., or "Optimistic Sales Figures", "Pessimistic Sales Figures", etc., etc.) and, by using the Scenario Manager dialog – choose Scenarios… from the TOOLS menu; the first time you use it, you may need to click on the down-arrows at the bottom of the menu first, to reveal it – easily compare the results of a number of different possible outcomes.

Use the Scenario Manager dialog box to try different scenarios in your Excel worksheets.

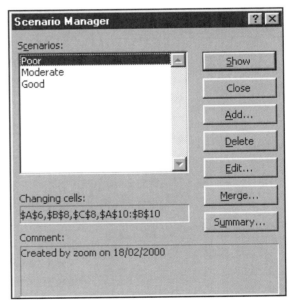

Scenarios can plug values into almost any part of Excel, though the scenarios themselves cannot contain formulas. They can even put values into one- and two-variable tables – allowing for multiple "What-If?" predictions using the same basic formulas – PivotTable source tables, and many other self-calculating items within Excel, making them extremely powerful.

CREATING AND VIEWING A SCENARIO

When you have a worksheet where you want to regularly change a number of data values, it is easy to set up and use a Scenario. Open the <u>Scenario Manager</u> by selecting <u>Scenarios</u> from the <u>TOOLS</u> menu as described on the previous page. Click <u>Add</u> to add a new Scenario. Enter a name for the Scenario and then enter the cell references for the cells that will be changed by the Scenario. Cells can be selected as normal. Click <u>OK</u>, and then enter the values that you want the cells to hold when this Scenario is selected using the form that opens. Click <u>OK</u> again. You can then repeat the process to add further Scenarios – after all, there's not much point having just one! To view the effect of any of your Scenarios, highlight its name and click on <u>Show</u>, or double-click on the name. The <u>Scenario Manager</u> will remain floating – and you will not be able to edit your worksheet – until you click <u>Close</u>.

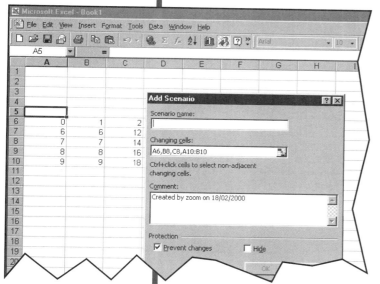

Add, delete or modify scenarios using the <u>Scenario Manager</u>.

To edit a Scenario, merely click <u>Edit</u> when the Scenario name is highlighted. Similarly, to delete a Scenario, highlight the Scenario name to be erased and click <u>Delete</u>. Clicking <u>Merge</u> will enable you to load Scenarios saved with another worksheet. <u>Summary</u> will create another worksheet in your workbook with a list of all the Scenarios, and the values they would substitute if effected.

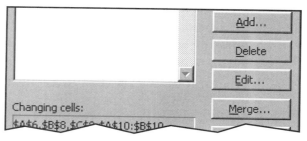

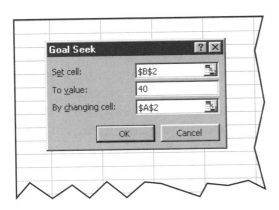

1 Set your <u>Goal Seek</u> parameters (above) and click on <u>OK</u> to perform a <u>Goal Seek</u>.

2 Your results will be displayed in a <u>Goal Seek Status</u> dialog box.

GOAL SEEK

The Goal Seeker and the Solver in Microsoft Excel are closely related, in that they both carry out a similar function – finding the value of one cell which makes another, related cell match some other specific value. The main difference between the two is the complexity of their operation. We'll look at the simpler of the two first – the Goal Seeker. Start the Goal Seeker by selecting <u>Goal Seek</u> from the <u>TOOLS</u> menu, revealed by clicking on the down arrows at the foot of the menu. The <u>Goal Seeker</u> dialog box will appear. Enter the reference of the cell that has to achieve the target value in the <u>Set Cell</u> text entry box (the cell should contain an equation), and the value that it has to reach in the <u>To Value</u> box. In the <u>By Changing Cell</u> box, enter the reference for the cell which Excel can try different values in to achieve the correct result. Then click <u>OK</u>. Excel will try putting different values into the changing cell until the equation in the target cell gives a value as close as it can to the answer you require.

SOLVER

The Solver is a more complex, more controllable (and more confusing) way of achieving the same end. The Solver is an Excel Add-In. If it doesn't appear in your <u>TOOLS</u> menu, after clicking on the down arrows at the menu foot, (as Solver) you will need to install it. Its operation is beyond the scope of this book, but you will be able to get full details from the Excel help system.

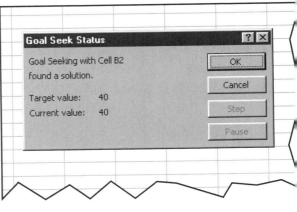

The <u>Solver</u> offers even more advanced functions.

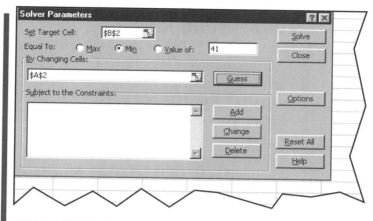

The <u>Analysis ToolPak</u> is another Excel Add-in that you may wish to add.

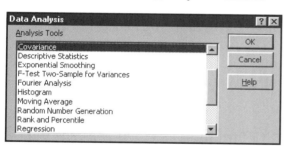

THE ANALYSIS TOOLPAK

The Analysis ToolPak is an Excel Add-In. If it doesn't appear in your <u>Tools</u> menu as <u>Data Analysis</u> you will need to install it, by clicking on <u>Add-Ins</u> on the <u>Tools</u> menu. A dialog box will appear with available add-ins; check the box beside <u>Analysis ToolPak</u> and click <u>OK</u>. The Analysis ToolPak contains many in-depth statistical functions, most of which would take a book all on their own to cover properly.

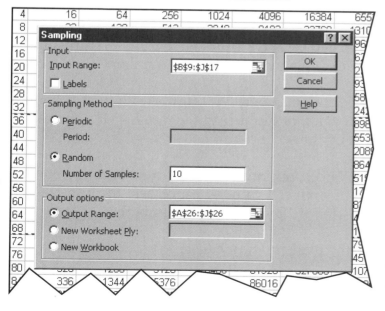

On selecting any analysis method, a dialog box will appear enabling you to set various factors and parameters, and select the section of data in a worksheet that you want to analyse. You can also select whether the analysis report will appear in the current worksheet, or whether a new worksheet will be created to display it. Installing the Analysis ToolPak adds a comprehensive section to the Excel Help system that will enable you to explore the tools further.

BUILT-IN FUNCTIONS

Excel provides many built-in functions to enable you to do arithmetical, statistical and financial calculations on the data in your worksheets. There is a complete list of functions between pages 117 and 120, but the ones listed below are some of the most important functions for data analysis, and include a brief description.

SUM(cell ref1 : cell ref2) OR (number1, number2, etc...) – to add a range of cells between cell ref1 and cell ref2 inclusive.

INT(cell ref) OR (number) – returns just the whole number (integer) part of the contents of cell ref or the number.

AVERAGE(cell ref1 : cell ref2) OR (number, etc ...) – returns the average value of a range of cells or numbers.

STDEV(cell ref1 : cell ref2) OR (number, etc ...) – returns the standard deviation from the average of a range of cells or numbers.

MIN(cell ref1 : cell ref2) OR (number, etc ...) – returns the lowest number from a range of cells or numbers.

MAX(cell ref1 : cell ref2) OR (number, etc ...) – returns the highest number from a range of cells or numbers.

ROUNDUP(cell ref, number) OR (number, number) – rounds up the first cell value or number to the number of decimal places defined by the second number.

ROUNDDOWN(cell ref, number) OR (number, number) – rounds down the first cell value or number to the number of decimal places defined by the second number.

PI() – returns the mathematical constant π ("Pi") to 15 decimal places.

WORKING WITH DATA

Getting the most from your data means using Excel's versatility to work with other users effectively. There are lots of ways you can make your data accessible to others, from maintaining it as a simple database to sharing it over a network or even publishing it on the web. In this chapter, we'll have a look at the techniques of database construction and management, and at some of the methods of making your workbooks accessible to others.

9

DATABASES

Excel can be used to store information in the format of a list or database. A database consists of a number of records – represented in an Excel spreadsheet by a row – each of which contain information stored in a number of different fields, represented in Excel by a column. The most simple type of database is formed when you create a row of headings (the fields), and then fill in rows of information below them (the records). While it is possible for records to be read down in columns, with the headings being listed in the first column, this is extremely unusual, and will confuse certain of Excel's important functions. Certain more advanced database types – such as relational databases which store information in parallel regions – can be created using Excel, but Microsoft Access is more suited to that sort of work.

The database below uses row 2 as its header row.

	A	B	C	D	E
1					
2	Salesman	Region	Month	Product	Sales
3	Connery	North	January	Sheep	5345
4	Robards	West	February	Cats	654
5	Donovan	Central	March	Dogs	53
6	Priestley	East	April	Sporks	7721
7	Newstead	South	May	Things	7859
8					
9					
10					
1					

HEADER ROWS

The header rows indicate the field names of your database categories. Excel uses them to refer to all of the information in a particular column and, within a record, to a particular piece of information. You also use them to quickly find the cell or piece of information you require. When you are designing a database, try to think ahead to all the different pieces of information you are going to need to categorize. If you want to make a database of your clients, you will need their names, full addresses, phone, fax, mobile and email details. However, if you want to prepare letters for them, you are going to need to hold a field for how you start the letter too – Dear <honorific> <surname> isn't going to do for everyone. Thinking ahead will save you a lot of hassle.

USING A FORM TO ENTER DATA

Along with entering data directly into a worksheet under the relevant columns, Excel offers a simple, but effective, form facility. It is accessible from the <u>DATA</u> menu, by selecting the <u>Form</u> option. It only works if you have a header row in your database. Click on a cell in the header row of your database and select the <u>Form</u> option from the <u>DATA</u> menu. The <u>Form</u> dialog box will appear on the screen, allowing you to enter records into your database in a form-based manner. A text entry box will appear on the <u>Form</u> dialog box for each field in your header row, beside the field name. If you have no records in your database, these text entry boxes will be blank. If you already have data in your database, they will contain the information from the first record. Also, seven buttons will appear on the right side of the <u>Form</u> dialog box.

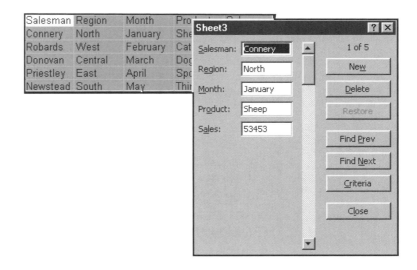

To add a new record to your database, press the <u>New</u> button, fill in all the relevant text entry boxes and click <u>New</u> again – the record will be placed at the end of your database. The <u>Delete</u> button will discard the current record and move all the records below it in the table up one line. If you alter any fields in a record and then decide you want to keep the original information, click on the <u>Restore</u> button. If you've changed some information and click on the <u>New</u> button, the altered information will replace the original information and the text entry boxes will clear, giving you the opportunity to add a new record. The <u>Find Prev</u> and <u>Find Next</u> buttons move through the database – the number of the record you are viewing is shown at the top of the <u>Form</u> dialog box.

Use the <u>Criteria</u> box to search through your records.

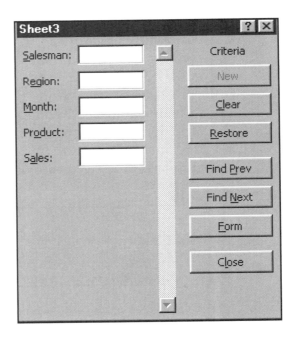

The <u>Criteria</u> button alters the function of the <u>Form</u> dialog box – it allows you to filter the records that appear in the <u>Form</u> dialog box by matching criteria you enter into the text entry boxes and then using the <u>Find Prev</u> and <u>Find Next</u> buttons. Clicking the <u>Close</u> button closes the <u>Form</u> dialog box and returns you to the worksheet.

DATA TYPES AND ACCEPTABLE VALUE

You can make sure that only the right kind of information is put into a field on your database using the <u>Validation</u> option on the <u>Data</u> menu. You can also define prompts that will appear when a user tries to enter data into a certain field and error messages that will appear if they enter invalid information. Select a whole column – corresponding to the field that you want to validate entries for – then select the <u>Validatation</u> entry from the <u>Data</u> menu.

In the <u>Allow</u> dropdown control you can select from <u>Any Value</u>, <u>Whole Number</u>, <u>Decimal</u>, <u>List</u>, <u>Date</u>, <u>Time</u>, <u>Text Length</u> or <u>Custom</u>. <u>Any Value</u> is the default and allows anything to be entered into that field. <u>Whole Number</u>, <u>Decimal</u>, <u>Date</u>, <u>Time</u> and <u>Text Length</u> will make sure that the entry is of the chosen type. You can then choose whether the entry must fall between certain constraints, is equal to a certain figure, or more than or less than a certain figure. <u>List</u> allows you to check the entry against a specific entries in a list held elsewhere on your worksheet. The range of cells containing the list must be entered into the <u>Source</u> text entry box. You also have the option of showing a dropdown box of the list options when entering data into a list-validated cell. <u>Custom</u> allows you to judge, by formula (see Chapter Eleven) whether an outcome is true or false. The validation will only pass if the calculation of the formula produces a TRUE result. The second and third tabs of the <u>Validation</u> dialog box allow you to set the prompts displayed when the user is about to enter information (the prompt), and when the wrong sort of data for the field has been entered (the error message) for the field you are validating.

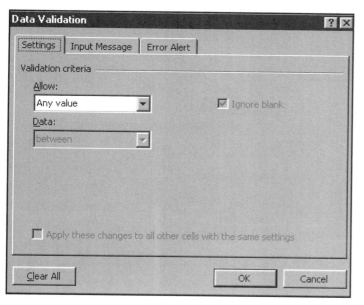

SORTING ON MULTIPLE COLUMNS

You can easily sort a database by selecting the Sort option on the DATA menu. Select a cell in your database range, and Excel will automatically try to judge and select the whole of the database before opening the Sort dialog box. If you have a header row in your database, Excel will not select it for sorting (it will use it to provide headings), though you have the option to override this using the radio buttons on the Sort dialog box.

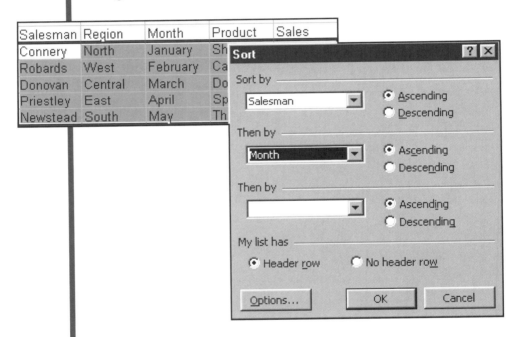

Excel gives you the ability to sort your database down to three levels. For instance, if you have a database of salesmen, the products they sell and the total sales they've made, you could tell Excel to sort it so that all sales by each salesman were grouped together, and within that, sales figures for each product would be grouped together, and then, within each product, the sales figures could be sorted from highest to lowest. You can produce different nested sorts in this manner by choosing different sort orders, and varying whether data is sorted in ascending or descending order.

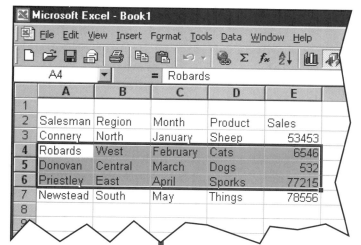

SORTING SECTIONS OF A LIST

You can sort just a section of your database by highlighting the rows you wish to sort before selecting the <u>Sort</u> option from the <u>Data</u> menu.

Excel will not be able to read the header rows when you are sorting only a section of your database, so the <u>Sort</u> dialog box will refer to each column as Column A, Column B and so on.

By combining localized sorts of this kind with careful use of general sorts, it is possible to generate some extremely sophisticated sort orders for your data structures, should this prove necessary – such as when a particular subset of information is required for export to a different program or function, for example.

1 Highlight a small section of your data (above) and use <u>Sort</u> from the <u>Data</u> menu to sort it by various criteria (right).

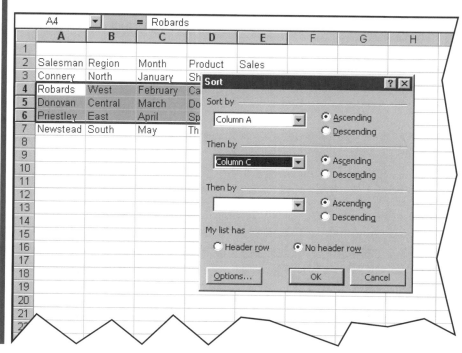

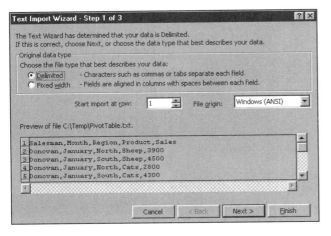

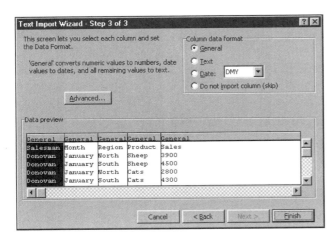

THE IMPORT TEXT FILE WIZARD

You may receive a spreadsheet file from a colleague or friend in a format not directly recognized by Excel. A number of industry-standard formats exist, but the most common is .CSV ("Comma Separated Values", or "Comma Delineated Format"). Excel provides an option for opening these files (and variants thereof) in the Text Import Wizard, which will open automatically when an unrecognized file format is encountered. Most databases can save files in CSV format, so it is also a useful method of getting data into Excel from a different database application.

When you open it, the Text Import Wizard will try to guess what's going on. Often the default options it chooses are correct, so you can often just click on Next to go to Step 2.

In the second image, Excel has guessed incorrectly – the file is comma-delimited, not tab-delimited, so just select Comma, deselect Tab and click Next again.

Step 3 (pictured left)allows you to set the format of data being imported – useful if you have special fields such as dates or number fields that need to be treated as plain text while being imported. Phone numbers, for example, often get translated to Scientific Notation format if not specifically imported as plain text. If everything is as you want, click on Finish.

QUERIES

Queries enable you to import information from external databases using standard database connections, such as Microsoft Access, SQL or ODBC. You can also use Web Query to access databases across the Internet. You access queries through the Get External Data option on the DATA menu.

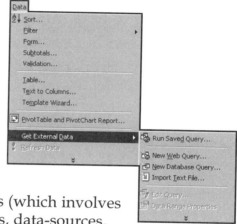

While it is out of the scope of this book to discuss creating queries (which involves knowledge of databases, data-sources, linkages and query languages), Microsoft Excel does provide some pre-written queries (particularly web queries), including access to Dow Jones stock exchange figures and a query which will search the Internet for more pre-written queries. The New Web Query dialog box is shown below.

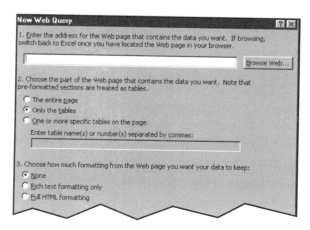

SHARING DATA

There are going to be instances when you will want other users to be able to access the data you have prepared, or when you yourself need access to other people's information. Even small businesses often have computer networks now, and they are vital for larger companies. While the specific details of networking and remote access are beyond the scope of the book, in this section we'll have a look at some of the ways that data may be shared.

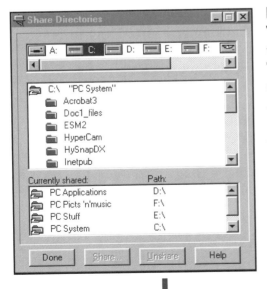

NETWORK FILES

The most common way of making a file available to more than one person is through a network. This means that although the workbook exists on just one computer, more than one person can access it and make changes to it. Networked data may be held on a specially-dedicated network drive – usually physically located on a Network Server computer, often to be found inside an IT department – or it may be held on one user's personal machine, but with access available to other users. If you are responsible for creating a document that will be used and updated over a network by several people, it is often worth unlocking just the cells that will need updating and then protecting the worksheet, as discussed elsewhere.

BUSY FILES

If a file requires regular updates from several people – a sales ledger, customer information list, or other such document – then it is important not to let more than one person modify the file at a time, to avoid data loss. Almost all networks are able to change a document's readability once it is already being accessed by one person so that if it is already in use, other people will be unable to open it.

SHARED WORKBOOKS

A better option, if you are going to regularly need to have different people work on a workbook is to enable Sharing. This allows up to 256 different users to access and modify a workbook simultaneously, keeping track of all the individual changes and the most current information.

1 To make a Shared work-book, select <u>Share Workbook</u>… from the <u>TOOLS</u> menu.

2 On the <u>Editing</u> tab, click the button marked <u>Allow changes by more than one user at the same time</u>.

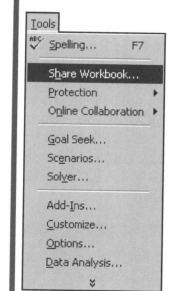

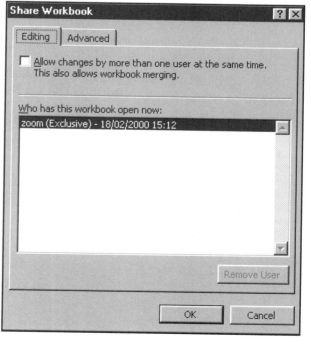

TRACKING WORKBOOK CHANGES

When you enable Sharing on a workbook, Excel automatically sets up a historical record of the changes made to the workbook, recording not only what was changed, but also the user who made the changes, and the date that they were made. In order to stop the workbook getting too big, only changes made in the last 30 days are actually stored, although this time limit can be modified. You can change this figure from the <u>Advanced</u> tab of the <u>Share Workbook</u> dialog. Another useful option that you may want to implement is to have Excel check the workbook for changes made by other users (and to inform others of your changes) at regular intervals, rather than when the workbook is saved, which is the default. Of course, if you're following good practice and saving your files regularly, there is little practical difference.

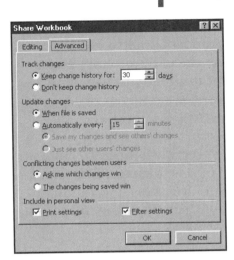

Set up how changes to a worksheet will be tracked in the <u>Share Workbook</u> dialog box...

It is also possible to have Excel highlight the changes that have been made by other users when it updates the workbook. This can be invaluable if several people are working with the same general area of a worksheet. To activate this, select <u>Track Changes</u> from the <u>TOOLS</u> menu (you may have to click on the down-arrows at the foot of the menu to reveal this option) and click on the <u>Highlight Changes...</u> option. In the <u>Highlight Changes</u> dialog box, tick the <u>Track Changes While Editing</u> selection, and click <u>OK</u>.

... you can see exactly who is making which changes to the worksheet as well.

REVIEWING CHANGES

There are three different major ways you can review the changes made to a workbook. The most commonly used option is to view the alterations made by other people since the last time you saved. From the <u>Highlight Changes</u> dialog box, ensure the <u>When</u> box is ticked, and select <u>Since I Last Saved</u> from the <u>When</u> pick-list. You can then either view the changes in a yellow notes box cell-by-cell when you run the pointer over that cell by selecting <u>Highlight changes on screen</u>, or you can read a full list in a <u>History</u> worksheet added temporarily to your workbook by selecting <u>List changes on a new sheet</u>.

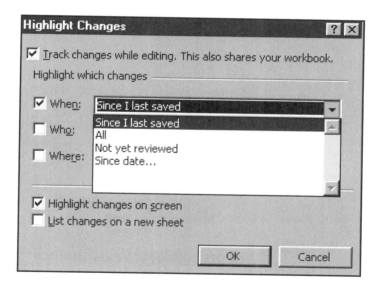

By selecting different options from the <u>When</u>, <u>Who</u> and <u>Where</u> pick-lists in the same dialog, it is possible to specify for a specific date, user or range of cells – or a combination of the above. Finally, by selecting <u>All</u> from the <u>When</u> box pick-list, and deselecting the <u>Who</u> and <u>Where</u> boxes, it is possible to get a list of all changes made to the workbook within the entire change history.

CONVERTING A WORKSHEET TO HTML

The basic principles of publishing a spreadsheet or workbook as a web file are extremely simple. Providing that the information is not interactive – in other words, that you are just presenting the data in a worksheet as a static image – then all you have to do is choose to save your worksheet as HTML. Immediately before you do so, always save the file normally so that you can still gain access to the details of the file, because the conversion process will only preserve the material that is visible to the user, and not items like cell formulas or worksheet settings.

1 From the <u>FILE</u> menu, choose the <u>Save As Web Page...</u> option. The <u>Save As...</u> dialog will appear. Select either the <u>Entire Workbook</u> or <u>Selection: Sheet</u> radio button.

2 ... or select the <u>Publish</u> button to get the <u>Publish As Web Page</u> dialog box.

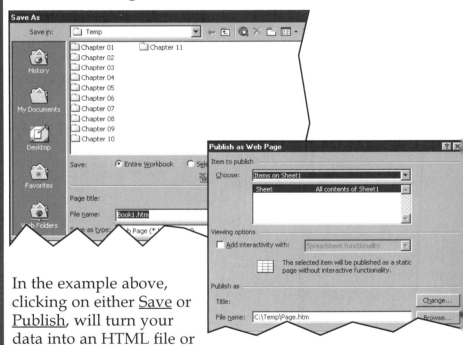

In the example above, clicking on either <u>Save</u> or <u>Publish</u>, will turn your data into an HTML file or files. If multiple web pages are required – such as to provide details of different worksheets – then a properly-linked folder will be created along with the HTML file so that the different elements of data referred to can be accessed in a web browser. Because some elements do not necessarily appear exactly as they do on the screen, it is always worth checking your new web material by loading it into your browser before you publish it properly on the web.

INTERACTIVE WEB PUBLISHING

Interactive web data allows a web user to manipulate and work with your information via a web page. The different types of interactivity provide slightly different functions, but will allow a web user to do things like filtering, personalizing data for a calculation, or using summary and analysis tools. Users must be running Microsoft Office Web Components and Microsoft Internet Explorer 4.01 or later in order to be able to view interactive data that you put up. If you want to be able to reach as many people as possible with your data, stick to non-interactive formats; if you are certain that the people viewing the data are going to be set up with MS Office Web Components and recent versions of Internet Explorer, then go ahead with interactive formatting.

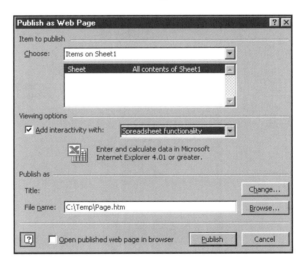

Whether you are working with the <u>Publish Web Page</u> dialog or the <u>Save As...</u> dialog, to add interactivity to your data tick the <u>Add Interactivity</u> box. Note that this is not available if you wish to save the entire workbook. If you are saving the whole sheet, just one mode of Interactivity is available to you, Spreadsheet mode. If you choose to Publish a specific object or range, you can also select <u>PivotTable Interactivity</u> or <u>Chart Interactivity</u>. As the names suggest, these three options are suitable for their respective object types.

SAVING TO AN FTP SITE

FTP – short for File Transfer Protocol – is an internet tool for transferring files between computers that may be anywhere around the world. Microsoft Excel allows you to treat specific FTP-able locations (called FTP Sites) as another part of your hard drive or network. This lets you save files directly to an FTP site. One important use of this is to publish your web-based data directly onto your web site, as most web sites are updated, and the files that make them up accessed, by FTP.

1 To save a file to FTP, you first need to tell your machine where to look. In the <u>Save As...</u> dialog box, click on the <u>Save In</u> pick-list. Select <u>FTP Locations</u>, and an option called <u>Add/Modify FTP Locations</u> will be displayed, along with a list of locations.

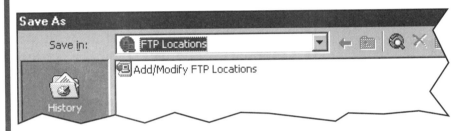

2 Either double-click the FTP site to publish to, or double-click on the <u>Add/Modify FTP Locations</u> option and configure the site details. Clicking on <u>OK</u> will make your computer connect to the location specified.

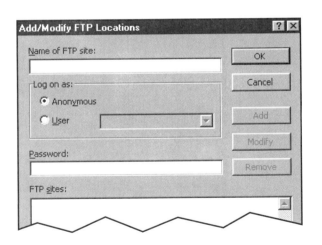

3 Once you are connected to the FTP site, the <u>Save As...</u> dialog box will allow you to navigate the FTP site in the same way as any part of your own hard drive. Once you have located the authorized place to save your file, you may do so as normal – although backups will not be created on your system until you re-save the workbook on your own computer again.

CUSTOMIZE EXCEL

Although Excel goes out of its way to make things as easy for the user as possible, not everyone is completely happy with the layout and functions available. Microsoft have thought of a way to help you get around that too – customization. You can change around the icons and toolbars to get them exactly the way you want, and you can even create entirely new sub-programs and functions, called Macros, to make tasks you repeat often that bit more convenient. This last chapter will cover the ways you can make your copy of Excel your very own.

CUSTOMIZING THE TOOLBARS

There are a number of useful things you can do to change the configuration of the toolbars that Excel displays. The Toolbars themselves are a great time-saving resource, and often include options that are not quite the same as their menu item counterparts. The <u>New Document</u> button on the toolbar for example automatically creates a new blank standard worksheet, while the <u>New...</u> menu option from the <u>FILE</u> menu opens up a dialog box for you to choose a new document template from. If there are menu functions that you use a lot of the time, you may want to consider adding buttons for them to your toolbars.

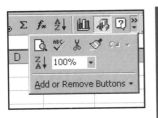

If you don't like floating buttons you can "raft" your toolbars.

RAFTING THE STANDARD AND FORMATTING TOOLBARS

If you don't always use Excel in full-screen mode, having the Standard and Formatting toolbars on one line can get inconvenient. The buttons that would normally fall off the edge of the window are still accessible by clicking the small continuation chevrons at the end of the bar, but that is not necessarily convenient. You can tell Excel to place the toolbars on separate lines to gain great accessibility to the icons.

Click on the <u>Customize...</u> option on the <u>TOOLS</u> menu, and select the <u>Options</u> tab of the <u>Customize</u> dialog. Under <u>Personalized Menus and Toolbars</u>, deselect <u>Standard And Formatting Toolbars Share One Row</u>, and click <u>OK</u>. The two toolbars will be switched to separate rows.

POSITIONING THE TOOLBARS

It is possible to move the toolbars around to different positions on the screen according to your needs and preferences. Each toolbar has a default position, including ones that are not automatically displayed at startup, and it may be useful to change those positions from time to time.

Every toolbar that is part of the screen borders, including the menu bar, begins with a small line across the width of the bar. This is the handle by which you can pick up the toolbar and move it around. When the cursor runs over the line, it changes to a four-directional cross-like arrow. At this point, you can click and hold the mouse button to drag the toolbar around the screen. Toolbars can switch between three different modes, a horizontal bar (the default for the major bars) which is activated by moving the bar to the top or bottom edge of the window, a vertical bar, which is activated when you move a bar onto the left-hand edge of the window, and a floating palette, activated by moving the bar away from the edges. In addition, floating palettes can be resized through a number of standard sizes by clicking on the edges and resizing them as you would a window. If you aren't happy with the effect you achieve, you can move the toolbar back to its old position easily.

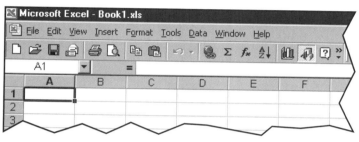

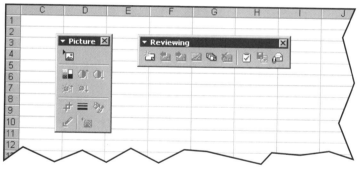

The three types of toolbar: horizontal (top), floating (middle) and vertical (right).

1 Select <u>Customize...</u> from the <u>TOOLS</u> menu.

2 The <u>Customize</u> dialog box will appear. Make sure the <u>Toolbars</u> tab is selected.

ADDING NEW TOOLBARS
There are several toolbars that are not displayed as part of the standard setup. Some of these are activated by clicking on icons on the standard toolbar, such as the Drawing icon, while others are activated by selecting a particular type of object, such as the Chart toolbar. You can also manually select and deselect all the different toolbars available to the program.

3 Scroll down the list to find the toolbars you want to add or hide, and tick or clear the boxes as appropriate. As you do so, the toolbars will appear or disappear. When you are happy, click <u>OK</u>.

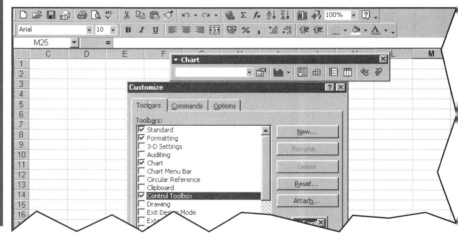

AUTOMATIC TOOLS

Although it is possible to deselect all the toolbars completely, including the menu bar, Excel will restore the Menu bar once you close the dialog box, to make sure you can still use the program.

ADDING AND MOVING BUTTONS

In addition to changing the range of different toolbars accessible to you and their positions on the screen, you can also modify which buttons appear within a specific toolbar. From the <u>Customize</u> dialog box, make sure the <u>Commands</u> tab is selected.

To remove a button from a toolbar, click on the button and keep the mouse held (the button will be surrounded by a black box), then drag the button off the toolbar. A small cross will appear in the box, and if you let go of the mouse, the button will be deleted.

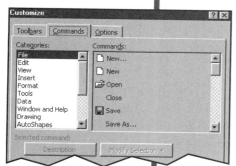

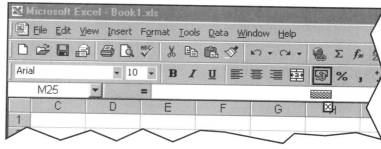

Open the <u>Customize</u> dialog box to add, move or delete icons and menu entries.

To move a button to a new location (including on a new toolbar), click on it and drag it to its new location. The insertion point will be indicated by a black insertion mark at the point where the button will move to. Buttons cannot be placed on top of each other. Marking a button as <u>Begin A Group</u> (from the right-click pop-up menu) puts a small grey bar in front of the button.

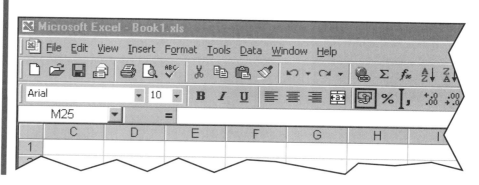

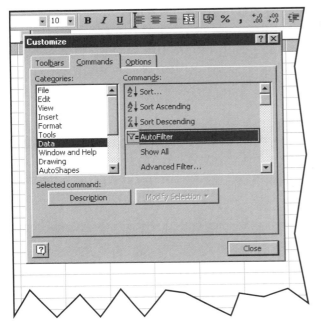

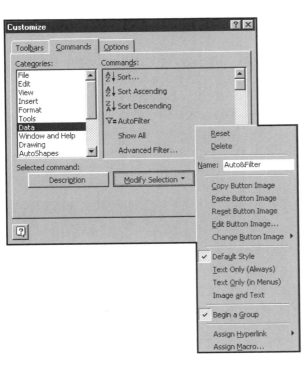

CREATING A NEW BUTTON

To add a button, you need to select the appropriate command from the Command tab of the <u>Customize</u> dialog box. Click on the list of menu titles in the left-hand list, and all the commands that fall under that category will be displayed in the right hand list by name and icon. Macro commands that you have created will be displayed under the Macro heading. Click and drag the command you wish to use onto the appropriate menu bar, which will expand (as much as possible) to accommodate it. If the command has an icon, that will be displayed as the new button, otherwise the name will be displayed.

Once in place however, a button image can be modified. Click on the button you wish to change, and then click the <u>Modify Selection</u> button. The Modify menu will appear.

Click on the <u>Change Button Image</u> selection, and a small palette of icon options will be shown to you. You may select one for the button you are modifying. Alternatively, you can click on the <u>Edit Button Image</u> selection to call up the <u>Button Editor</u>. Click on a colour and then on a square in the large-scale image to change a pixel in the 16x16 grid. The <u>Erase</u> character is shown as transparent in the final button. When you are happy with the final button, click <u>OK</u>, and your custom button image will be applied.

CREATING A NEW TOOLBAR

Creating a new toolbar lets you collect together a range of the buttons and commands that you use most frequently in one place without altering the basic layout of the program – very handy if you are not the only person using the machine.

1 From the Toolbars tab of the Customize palette, select the New... button. This is different to the New and New... icons on the Commands tab, which are the commands for starting a new document.

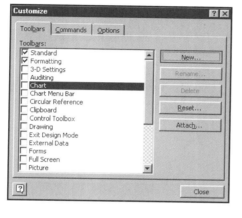

2 In the New Toolbar dialog that appears, type in a name for the new toolbar, and click OK.

3 The new toolbar will be added as a floating bar with one single blank space, next to the Customize palette, and it will also be added to the bottom of the list in the Toolbars tab of the pallete.

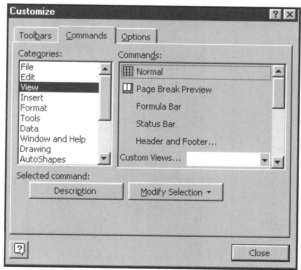

4 Drag commands onto the new toolbar from the Commands tab as required. The new toolbar will expand to fit the items you wish to include. You can then leave it floating, or attach it to a border.

1 Activate the Customize palette.

CHANGING MENUS
Modifying menus is exactly the same as modifying toolbars.

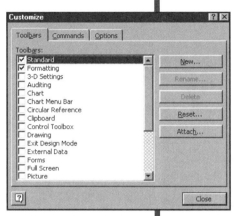

2 Click on a menu and release the button. The menu will stay open. Do not click and drag on the menu unless you wish to move or delete it entirely.

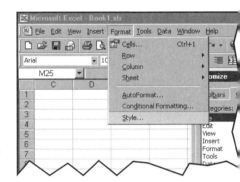

3 Click on the menu item to be removed, and drag it off the menu into the screen to delete it...

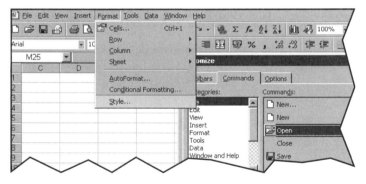

4 ...or drag an item from the Commands tab to add it to the menu, in the position you place it.

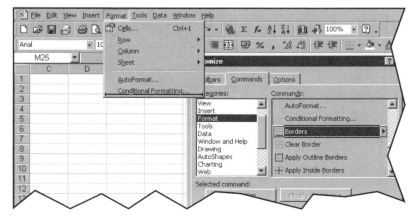

1 Once you have created your custom toolbar, open the Customize... dialog box, and the workbook that you want to attach the custom toolbar to, and select the custom toolbar from the Toolbars tab.

2 Click the Attach... button, and the Attach Toolbars dialog box will appear.

3 Select the custom toolbar you want to attach to the open workbook, from the list titled Custom Toolbars: on the left, and click Copy. The selected toolbar will now be listed in the Toolbars in Workbook box too. Now, when you save the workbook, the toolbar will be saved with it.

SAVING A CUSTOM TOOLBAR

By default, Excel will save all your custom toolbars for you in its default settings, so that your toolbars are always available on your machine. However, you can also tell it to save your custom toolbars with a workbook, so that a toolbar of commands you have specially prepared can be used by anyone who opens the document.

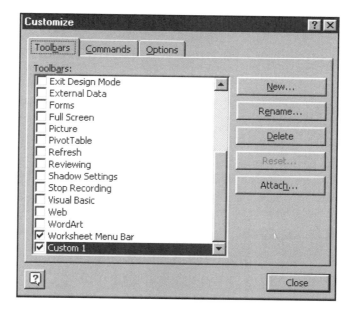

WORKING WITH MACROS

In this section you'll learn how to use macros to automate tasks within Excel. If you carry out any sort of repetitive activity, Excel macros can easily save you the bother of carrying out exactly the same sequences of key-presses, mouse movements and/or menu selections over and over again.

WHAT IS A MACRO?

A macro is a small program within Excel, which, when activated, affects a workbook or worksheet. Macros let you automate all sorts of tasks and can provide very advanced functions if you know how to program. Don't worry if you don't know how to write programs though. Excel can be told to "record" a sequence of events as you carry them out – opening a menu, selecting an item, clicking on a button and so on – and turn that recording into a macro.

The macro produced can then be added as a Custom toolbar button, given a special key shortcut, or opened in the <u>Macro Editor</u> and altered or enhanced.

To create a macro you have to "record" it. You can do this from within <u>TOOLS</u>.

WHAT SORTS OF THINGS CAN MACROS DO?

"Recorded" macros can mimic any user activity that takes place while the <u>Macro Record</u> facility is switched on. For instance, a macro could record the user selecting a column of cells, and clicking on the <u>Sort Alphabetically</u> button on the tool bar. Whenever that particular macro was run, the same column (or, depending on the macro settings, whichever column the selected cell was in) would automatically be sorted in alphabetical order, even if it was not selected before, or even if it was not on-screen.

Macros can also record and playback dialog boxes being opened, receiving data, and being closed, or even swapping between workbooks. You can likewise record loading and saving data and moving cells around a sheet.

Macros are easy to generate with the <u>Macro Recorder</u> toolbar on your palette.

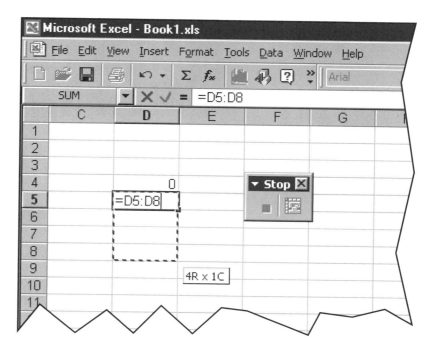

In fact, if you move beyond simply recording macros and write macros directly into the <u>Macro Editor</u>, you can get a macro to do almost anything, including the most complex calculations and data manipulation.

RECORDING A MACRO

Recording a macro is simple, but you must plan what you want to record before starting the <u>Macro Recorder</u> - if you make a mistake while recording a macro, that mistake will be recorded as well, so a little thought can save you some problems. Select the <u>Macro</u> item from the <u>TOOLS</u> menu, and click on <u>Record New Macro</u>. A dialog box will appear, allowing you to name your macro and decide where to store it. If this macro is only going to be of use to you in the current workbook, then select <u>This Workbook</u> in the <u>Store Macro In</u> text entry box. If you may want to use the macro with another worksheet, then select <u>Personal Macro Workbook</u>. You can also add a description of the macro here for later reference.

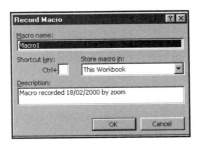

From the moment you click <u>OK</u>, the Macro Recorder will be working, so make sure you know exactly what you want to record.

When you click <u>OK</u>, a floating toolbar (above) will appear. If you want the macro to start from the current active cell, ensure that the <u>Relative Reference</u> button on the right of the floating toolbar is selected; if you want it to apply to the specific cells you choose, then deselect it. Now carry out whatever Excel activity you want to record and when you've finished, click the small blue square <u>Stop Recording</u> box in the floating toolbar, which ends recording.

THE MACRO DIALOG BOX

The <u>Macro</u> dialog box is accessed from the <u>Macros...</u> item on the <u>Macro</u> submenu of the <u>TOOLS</u> menu. It is from here that you can run macros, edit or delete them, or alter the macro options.

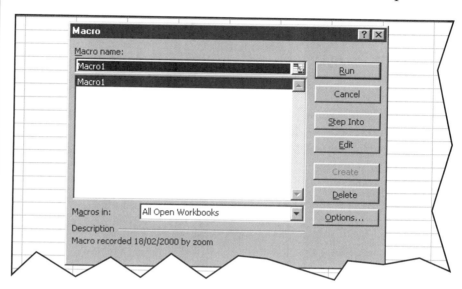

Run macros that you have already created from the Macro dialog box by pressing <u>Run</u>.

To run a macro that you have previously recorded, highlight its name in the <u>Macro</u> dialog box and click <u>Run</u> (or double-click on the name). The macro will run and the <u>Macro</u> dialogue box will disappear. <u>Step Into</u> and <u>Edit</u> will both open the Visual Basic for Applications Development Environment, where you can actually directly write the code for a macro. <u>Step Into</u> will run the first command in the macro, and is used for debugging a macro that isn't working as it is supposed to, while <u>Edit</u> just brings up the macro code for you to tinker with. The Visual Basic Environment is extremely complex and powerful, and beyond the scope of this work.

If you enter a name in the <u>Macro name</u> text entry box that doesn't correspond to a macro, you can then click on <u>Create</u> – that will start the Visual Basic for Applications Development Environment, allowing you to write a new macro from scratch. Clicking on <u>Delete</u> when a macro name is highlighted will delete that macro. <u>Options</u> allows you to change the macro description or shortcut key.

KEY SHORTCUTS FOR MACROS

When you record a macro, you can assign a <u>Shortcut Key</u> to the macro. This is a letter from the keyboard, which you press at the same time as the <u>Ctrl</u> key. Once a <u>Shortcut Key</u> has been assigned, you can simply press the shortcut combination and the macro will execute, without needing to open the <u>Macro</u> dialogue box.

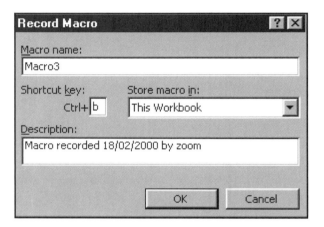

Choose your <u>Shortcut Key</u> carefully, as it will override the normal <u>Ctrl</u> key combination while it is active. For instance, the example above will stop you using <u>Ctrl-B</u> shortcut to set bold text until the worksheet that contains your <u>Ctrl-B</u> macro is unloaded. You can alter the <u>Shortcut Key</u> assigned to a macro (or add one to a macro without one) by selecting the <u>Options</u> button from the <u>Macro</u> dialog box when the macro name you wish to alter is highlighted. As there is no direct way of adding a <u>Shortcut Key</u> to a macro written directly through the Visual Basic for Applications Development Environment, this is the only way to assign a <u>Shortcut Key</u> to such a macro.

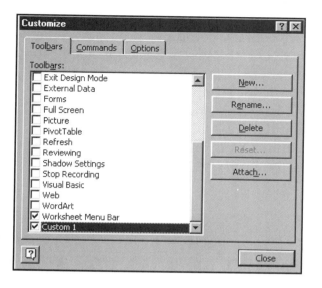

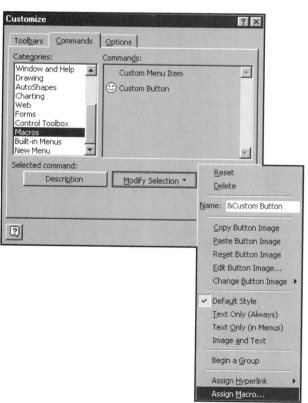

ADDING A MACRO TO A TOOLBAR

To increase the accessibility and convenience of accessing certain macros, you can add a new button to a toolbar that will execute the macro automatically when pressed. Select the Customize… item from the TOOLS menu. If the toolbar that you want to add a button to is not visible on your screen, click on the Toolbars tab and then select the toolbar you want to see by clicking in the checkbox beside the name of the toolbar.

Next, select the Commands tab from the Customize dialogue box and highlight the Macro selection in the Categories list box. Then drag the Custom button icon (the smiley face) to the toolbar you want the new button on. Click the Modify Selection button and select Assign Macro from the menu that appears. This will open the Assign Macro dialogue box. Select the macro you wish to assign to your custom button and click OK.

From the Modify Selection button, you can also change the image that appears on the button by selecting the Change Button Image item and choosing a new icon. You can repeat this process for as many buttons as you wish to add, clicking on Close on the Customize dialog box when you've finished.

MACROS AND VISUAL BASIC

Macros in Excel 2000 are actually computer programs, whether you write them line by line in the Visual Basic for Applications Development Environment or record them using the Record Macro facility. Visual Basic for Applications (VBA) is a powerful programming language and is a subset of Microsoft's industry-standard Visual Basic. Using VBA, you can make Excel do anything, from simply repeating a set of actions, to performing like a fully blown program using Excel's functionality.

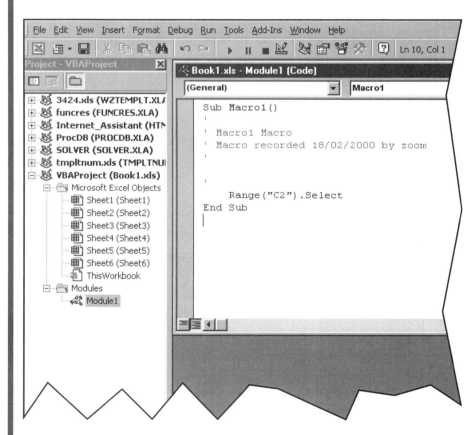

VBA Macros can be run from the Visual Basic for Applications Development Environment by selecting <u>Run Macro</u> from the <u>Run</u> menu, or by pressing <u>F5</u>, or by clicking on the <u>Run</u> icon (the small blue wedge) on the toolbar.

ADDING CODE TO A MACRO

While it is beyond the scope of this book to teach you to develop your own Visual Basic for Applications (VBA) macros, we can quickly look at how to examine and add code to a macro that you've recorded using the <u>Record Macro</u> function of Excel. To open the VBA Development Environment, select the <u>Visual Basic Editor</u> option from the <u>Macros</u> item on the <u>TOOLS</u> menu. Once the VBA Development Environment is open, select the <u>Macros</u> item from its <u>Tools</u> menu – this will open a dialog box identical in function to the <u>Macro</u> dialog box in Excel. From here you can select the Macro you want to load and click <u>Edit</u>. The Macro will appear in a window in the VBA Development Environment, showing you the code that was created automatically when you recorded the macro.

Using the Visual Basic Editor, you can adjust the Macros you have created.

From here, you can add or edit the code to alter the way the macro behaves. The Help system has a lot of information on developing VBA macros, or alternatively you could find a specific book on the subject. The power of VBA macros is immense, but don't let them scare you – simple repetitive functions can be automated to make your use of Excel even more easy. To close the VBA Development Environment, select <u>Close and Return to Excel</u> from the <u>File</u> menu. If you've made any changes to macros in this session, the VBA Development Environment will prompt you to save those changes before closing.

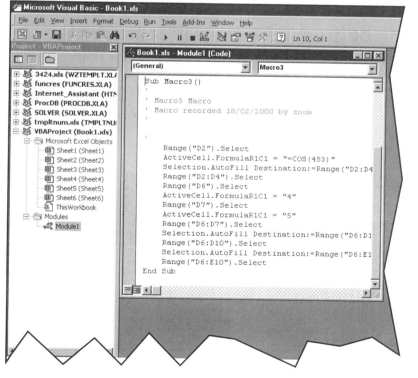

ADVANCED TOPICS

11

In this section, we'll look at some of the more important of the program's advanced aspects. First of all, the basic principles behind using Excel's built-in functions will be discussed. We'll also consider one particularly important set of functions, the IS Functions. Finally, we'll finish up by looking at what to do when functions don't seem to work, and grabbing a quick tour of what's changed in Excel since the last version.

FUNCTIONS

As mentioned earlier, a function is a small computer program built into Excel that performs a specific task, generally a calculation. In the following pages, we'll give you an introduction to the logic behind the way that functions are handled, as they are by far the most important of Excel's advanced functions.

LOGICAL SYNTAX

Computers in general are programmed using a standard system of logic that underpins the way they work. This has several consistent elements that you will need to know. The first is the way that decisions are made, using a system known as Boolean. In Boolean logic, things are either TRUE (represented by a 1) if the information you are checking (called an expression) is correct, or FALSE (represented by a 0) if it is not. In the picture to the left, the Boolean expression A1=5 is TRUE; the expression A2=9 is FALSE. Standard mathematical logical operators are also included, so + (plus), - (minus), * (multiply) and / (divide) all work in the usual mathematical way, as do = (equal to), < (less than), > (more than), <= (less than or equal to), >= (greater than or equal to) and <> (other than). That means that 2=3, 6<4, 3*3=8 and 5<>5 will always be FALSE.

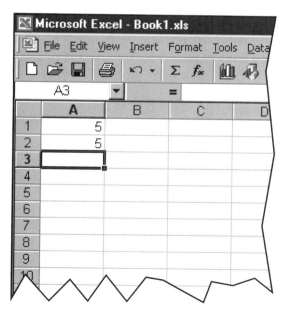

There are also several standard terms used in Boolean logic, used for comparing elements of an expression. These are <u>OR</u>, <u>AND</u> and <u>NOT</u>. <u>OR</u> sets an expression to TRUE if any one of its elements are TRUE. <u>AND</u> sets an expression to TRUE if all of its elements are TRUE. Finally, <u>NOT</u> sets an expression to TRUE if its argument is FALSE, like this:

ELEMENTS	OR	AND	NOT
0	FALSE	FALSE	TRUE
1	TRUE	TRUE	FALSE
0 and 0	FALSE	FALSE	-error-
0 and 1	TRUE	FALSE	-error-
1 and 0	TRUE	FALSE	-error-
1 and 1	TRUE	TRUE	-error-

INTRODUCTION TO VARIABLES

Like all programs, the various functions all work with **variables**. The name "variable" is a computing term, and means a value that can change – in other words, that can be variable. Functions can be extremely simple, or extremely complex, and so can the variables that they require. A function performs its calculations based on the variables that it has been given, and **returns** a **result**, two more pieces of computer jargon. For example, if a function takes two variables (eg. 2 and 3), collectively known as its **arguments**, and adds them together (like the SUM function does) its result – the value it returns – will be the total of those two variables (eg. 5).

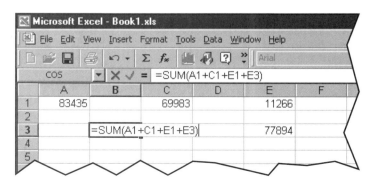

Excel functions insist on having their variables placed in brackets after the function name, and seperated by commas. This is always shown as follows: FUNCTIONNAME(Variable1,Variable2,Variable3…). As the previous example shows, when you can have as many variables as you like – as with the SUM function, which will add all the variables you pass it – this is shown with an ellipsis inside the variable brackets. They all share the same format, so even functions that do not have any variables, such as the one that tells you today's date, insist on being followed by brackets.

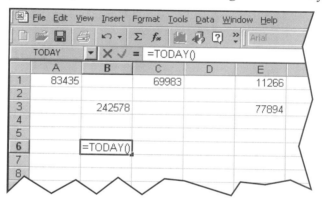

PASSING VARIABLES

Giving one or more variables to a function is known as **passing** them. Variables can be basic numbers, strings of text, cell names, cell range references, list items, dates, and just about anything else. Different functions can cope with different types of variables, enclosed within the brackets as normal.

TEXT VARIABLES

Passing a textual variable to a function is slightly different. To make sure that Excel understands that the variable is a piece of text, and that it should not be analysed as a numerical value, it has to be contained in "quotes". If you are passing more than one textual variable, each separate item should be in its own quotes, like this:

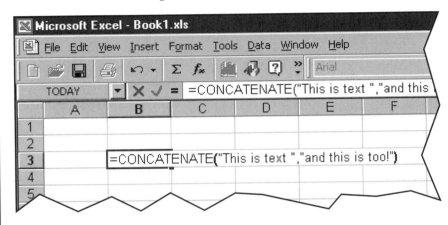

Until the function finds the closing quotes, it will assume every character (each individual letter, number, space or symbol) it encounters is part of the text of the variable – even a closing bracket. One entire text variable is called a **string**, another computing term. Functions that deal with the positions of a character within a string generally count from the left, and ignore the opening " sign. In other words, the fourth character in the string "ABCDEFGHIJKL" is D, not C, J or I.

CONDITIONAL TESTS

You can assign any logical test to a cell by putting an = in front of the expression. This is almost exactly the same as a cell formula, except that logical expressions are statements rather than calculations. These tests always return either TRUE or FALSE. For example, =A1>A2 will return TRUE if A1 is bigger and FALSE if A2 is bigger, or it A1 and A2 are the same. This is called a conditional test.

THE IF STATEMENT

Although it is by right a function itself, there is one specific tool available that allows you to analyse whether a logical expression is TRUE or FALSE, and give a different result depending on the answer. This is called the IF function, and its syntax is

=IF(Logical-_Expression,Result_if_True,Result_if_False). At its most basic, this can be extremely simple.

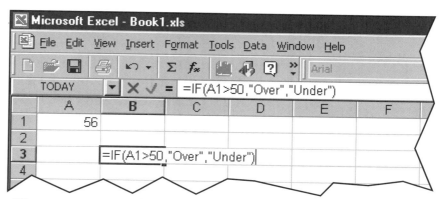

However, it can also get considerably more complicated. In the example above, the function will return the word Over if cell A1 holds 51 or more, and Under if it holds 50 or less. But what if you wanted a third case, for exactly on 50? Well, IF functions can be threaded together, like beads. In either of the IF statements result options, you can add another IF function (or one of several other functions). Stacking IF functions together like this is called nesting. An IF statement for the previous example would look like this:

=IF(A1>50,"Over", IF(A1=50,"Spot On","Under"))

That can be read aloud as "If A1 is more than 50 then the answer is 'Over' or else, if A1 is equal to 50 then the answer is 'Spot On', or else the answer must be 'Under'."

THE IS FUNCTIONS

There are a number of functions that test whether a variable – usually a cell reference, as that is the most practical use – is of a certain type. These all have the same format, ISTYPE(Variable), and they return TRUE if the variable is of the type specified, and FALSE if it is not of the type specified. If, for example, you had a form worksheet where a user had to enter a total in one particular cell, the ISNUMBER function could tell an IF statement whether that cell had a number in it – ie. =IF(ISNUMBER(A1),"OK","Enter Data!"). The IS Functions are used for different purposes: ISBLANK is TRUE if a cell is empty. ISEVEN, ISODD, ISNUMBER, ISTEXT and ISNONTEXT return TRUE if a cell holds data of that type, Even and Odd referring to numbers. ISLOGICAL checks to see if a cell contains either TRUE or FALSE (in which case it reports TRUE) or not (in which case it reports FALSE). Finally, ISERR, ISNA and ISERROR check to see if a cell holds an error message – any error except #N/A! for ISERR, only #N/A! for ISNA, and any error at all for ISERROR.

ERROR VALUES

As mentioned briefly on the previous page, Excel will display an error message in a cell when the program cannot properly evaluate a function or other cell formula. Some of the more basic errors are actually physically prevented by dialog boxes that tell you something you are attempting is wrong – such as trying to enter an invalid cell name, or trying to pass too many or too few variables to a function – but in other cases, the problem is beyond Excel's ability to notice at the time. In circumstances like these, Excel shows that something is wrong by displaying an Error Message in a cell. Understanding the significance of different error messages will help you considerably with working out why a formula is not behaving properly. It is important to remember that the problem may lie with one of the cells being referenced by your formula, and

ERROR	BASIC MEANING
#####	The number in this cell is too long to display.
#DIV/0!	The formula is trying to divide by 0, which is not possible.
#N/A!	A number needed to complete calculations is not available.
#NAME!	There is unrecognized text in this formula.
#NULL!	You have suggested a common area between two ranges without one.
#NUM!	A number you have entered is unacceptable.
#REF!	A cell reference is not valid.
#VALUE!	The formula has received the wrong type of argument.

also that you may have missed an important character, such as a speechmark for text or a closing bracket for a formula.

TROUBLESHOOTING ERRORS

Microsoft Excel's Help system has a number of special extended help topics dedicated to allowing you to perform a complicated task or correct a problem that has cropped up. Using these extended help topics is known as troubleshooting, because in the past it used to involve trying a number of different answers until you found the correct one – shooting at the trouble, so to speak. To get a list of relevant extended topics, type a keyword for your problem into the <u>Type Keywords</u> box of the <u>Index</u> tab within the help system, and follow it with the keyword troubleshoot. Then click on the <u>Search</u> button to get a list of help topics in the <u>Choose A Topic</u> box.

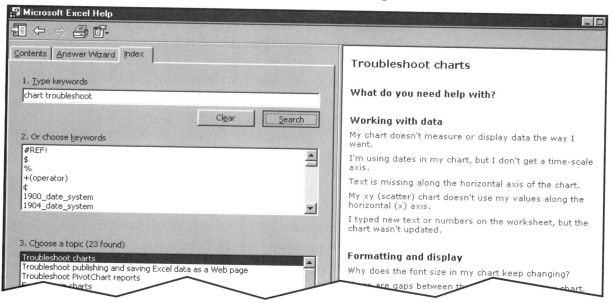

HELP FOR HELP

There are over 100 different troublshoot topics available to the Excel help system, so if you don't find the information you need immediately, try a different keyword to go with the troubleshoot keyword, or add another keyword relevant to your problem to cut down the number of topics displayed.

WHAT'S NEW IN EXCEL 2000

- Autofilling lists now includes formatting.
- Axis unit names can be scaled to be more appropriate for very large or very small numbers.
- Clip art functionality has been improved with the new version of the Clip Gallery.
- Cutting and Pasting has been enhanced with the multiple-item Office Clipboard.
- Four-digit year dates are now provided.
- Installing and maintaining Office has been made easier with a number of different improvements, such as making your settings transportable and providing auto-repair elements.
- Interactive PivotCharts are now provided.
- Macros can now be digitally signed to help improve security.
- Multiple language support is automatically provided.
- PivotTable functions have been greatly revised and expanded to make them simpler and more powerful.
- Save and Open have been enhanced with a new dialogue box and preset folder locations for convenient file grouping
- Self-customizing menu bars adjust to the options you most frequently use.
- The Office Assistant has stepped out of its box!
- Web functionality has been greatly expanded, including publishing data of all sorts of types to web page solutions, sharing web meetings, using office-specific formatting, providing international support, updating web queries, and enabling document subscriptions.
- Finally, several important development tools – such as the Visual Basic Editor and the Antivitus Support Suite – have been added or updated.

GLOSSARY

This book has been written using a minimum of technical terms. Nevertheless, you may have come across a few here and there. In case you had any problems with a particular term, this section contains definitions for some of the specialised words used within this book and in the Excel Help Files.

ABSOLUTE REFERENCE
A cell address in a formula which will not change if copied to another cell. Use a dollar sign ('$') infront of a row and/or column identifier to force it absolute.

ACTIVE WORKSHEET
The worksheet that you're working on in a workbook. The name on the tab of the active sheet is bold.

ADD-IN MACRO
A macro integrated into Excel that functions as if it were built into the application.

ARGUMENT
Information you supply to a function or calculation.

ARRAY
A rectangular area of cells sharing one common formula.

AXES

Lines bordering the plot area providing a frame of reference for measurement or comparison on a chart.

BOUND

A bound document can only appear in a single workbook. A bound document is saved in the workbook file.

CELL

The constituent boxes in an Excel spreadsheet, uniquely identified by a cell address, which make up the table.

CELL ADDRESS

The unique identifier of a cell, combining a column 'letter' with a row number.

CHART

A graphic representation of a segment of Excel data.

CLIPBOARD

The holding place for data you Cut or Copy, until it is Pasted or replaced by another piece of data.

COLUMN

A complete vertical line of cells, identified by a letter.

COMPARISON OPERATOR

One of the standard operators that returns a logical value.

=	Equal to
>	Greater than
<	Less than

>=	Greater than or equal to
<=	Less than or equal to
<>	Not equal to

CONSTANT
A number, text, logical or error value, that doesn't start with an equals sign ('=').

DOCUMENT
In Excel, a worksheet.

DATABASE
Part of a worksheet used for organizing, managing and retrieving information.

DATA TABLE
A range of cells summarizing the results of substituting different values into one or more formulas.

DATA SERIES
A group of related data points to be plotted on a chart.

EMBEDDING
Inserting data as an updatable object from another application.

EXPORTING
Saving data from Excel for use in another application.

EXTRACT RANGE
A separate area on a worksheet set aside for data retrieved and copied from a database.

EQUATION
A mathematical formula.

FIELD
A column or cell in a database.

FORMAT
The style that data is display within a cell.

FORMULA
The contents of any cell when those contents must be calculated and may change based upon the contents of other cells, or other factors such as a function.

FUNCTION
Predefined formulas that perform simple or complex calculations.

GRAPHIC OBJECT
A line or shape (button, text box, oval, rectangle, arc, picture) placed in your worksheet.

GRIDLINES
The dotted lines on the worksheet that separate the cells.

HANDLES
Small black squares located in the lower right-hand corner of selected cells or around selected graphic objects or chart items, used to move, resize or format the selected object.

IMPORTING
Introducing data into Excel from another application.

INPUT CELL
The cell into which values from a data table are inserted.

LINKED DOCUMENTS
Separate documents that are dynamically connected so that a formula in one document refers to a value in another document.

LINKING
Dynamic data exchange (DDE) between Excel documents and documents created in other applications, such as Microsoft Word.

LOGICAL VALUE
The result of a formula that contains a logical function or equation - Excel recognises both TRUE and FALSE and 1 and 0.

MACROS
Instructions that you create to automate certain tasks.

NAME
An identifier you create to refer to a cell, a group of cells, a constant value, an array of values or a formula.

OPERATOR
A symbol or function that, along with data, makes an equation.

PIVOT TABLE
An Excel tool which enables you to manipulate axes of a table or database interactively.

RECORD
One row in a database.

REFERENCE
See cell address.

RELATIVE REFERENCE
By default, all cell addresses are relative. A cell address in a formula will change to refer to another cell if it is moved to another cell.

ROW
A complete horizontal line of cells, identified by a number.

SCROLL BARS
Grey bars along the right and bottom sides of a worksheet that enable you to move off-screen areas of the worksheet into view.

SERIES FORMULA
A formula that contains the data used to plot a data series on a chart.

SPREADSHEET
The generic name for the type of application which Excel is; also the generic name for the method of storing data in a grid of cells.

STARTUP DIRECTORY
An optional directory named XLSTART which is located in the same directory as EXCEL.EXE. Documents placed in it are automatically loaded when Excel is started.

TAB
The 'filing system' style tags at the bottom left of the screen

which allow you to swap between worksheets in a workbook.

TABLE
The collection of cells within a worksheet which make up a spreadsheet.

TEMPLATE
A document created for use as a basic pattern or form for other similar documents.

TOOLS
Buttons on a toolbar; also a top-level menu containing useful functions.

TOOLBAR
A collection of tool buttons, normally docked at the top of the screen but able to float elsewhere.

UNBOUND
An unbound document can be a part of several workbooks and is saved in a separate file.

VBA
Microsoft's Visual Basic for Applications - the language macros are written in.

WORKBOOK
A collection of worksheets within a single file.

WORKSHEET
A single spreadsheet within an Excel workbook, often just 'sheet'.

WEB RESOURCES

There are hundreds of sites on the Internet where you can find Excel related information. Just typing "Excel 2000" into a search engine produces tens of thousands of hits. We've spent some time sifting through these to find the best sites for you to extend your Excel knowledge. We've categorized the sites into headings including Resources, where you'll find extensions and other useful things; Samples, where you'll find pre-coded worksheets and other material; Macros, where you'll find collections of macros written by others; and Help, where you'll find more useful advice.

RESOURCES

The first place to look for additional information is of course the Microsoft homepage, found at http://www.microsoft.com. This site is huge, but there is a very efficient search facility throughout and help, as for all Microsoft products, is available at the click of a button. It helps to know exactly what you need before going there though.

Microsoft is also the software company that produces your operating system, Windows. Windows has a feature called Windows update, accessible from the Start button. Let Windows check its configuration and update itself so that you are running the latest version.

UPDATES AND PRODUCT FIXES
http://www.microsoft.com/downloads

FONTS
Try one of the following for free fonts:
http://www.microsoft.com/typography/fontpack
http://www.fontfree.com

LANGUAGE ADD-ONS
http://msdn.microsoft.com/officedev/downloads/addon.asp

ENTERPRISE SUPPORT
http://www.microsoft.com/office/enterprise/entsupport.htm

CLIPART
In one of your favourite search engines, type "free clipart".
You will see that there are lots of sites dedicated to providing
you with free stuff. Most of these sites are private and all of
them are crammed with freebies, usually arranged by easy to
browse categories. http://www.clipartconnection.com is one
of them, along with http://www.artclipart.com. All these sites
have links to other freebies sites, so don't hesitate to have a
look around for that special piece of clip art. Clip art is usually
copyright free, but do make sure before you use it.

http://www.clipartconnection.com
http://www.artclipart.com
http://officeupdate.microsoft.com/2000/downloadDetails/cli
pgalv2000.htm

TRIAL PROGRAM ADD-INS
Amigo 2000 Charting Program:
http://officeupdate.microsoft.com/2000/downloadDetails/amigdemo.htm
JITI Builder:
http://officeupdate.microsoft.com/2000/downloadDetails/jbmsot.htm
Spreadsheet Assistant:
http://officeupdate.microsoft.com/2000/downloadDetails/Assistnt.htm
Monte Carlo Risk Simulator:
http://officeupdate.microsoft.com/2000/downloadDetails/esim50.htm
Report Runner: http://www.add-ins.com/runner.htm

TEMPLATES
Sample Templates:
http://officeupdate.microsoft.com/2000/downloadDetails/Template.htm
Chart & Spreadsheet Components:
http://officeupdate.microsoft.com/2000/downloadDetails/Owcsamps.htm
http://www.cpearson.com/excel.htm
http://www.setileague.org/software/spreadsh.htm
http://supershareware.co.uk/Apps/2615.asp

MACROS
http://officeupdate.microsoft.com/2000/downloadDetails/Recmrk2k.htm
http://www.BMSltd.co.uk/Excel/Default.htm
http://www.mindspring.com/~tflynn/excelvba.html
http://www.evirus.com
http://support1.pys.bris.ac.uk/excel/default.htm
http://www.dtiprinceton.com/excelmacropop.htm

HELP

http://support.microsoft.com/support/default.asp?PR=xlw2k&FR=0&SD=GN&LN=EN-US&

http://msdn.microsoft.com/resources/

http://officeupdate.microsoft.com/welcome/excel.asp

http://officeupdate.microsoft.com/2000/articlelist/ExcelTips.htm

http://officeupdate.microsoft.com/articlelist/o2kExcelarticles.htm

http://support.microsoft.com

http://www.microsoft.com/downloads/default.asp

WEB TOOLS

http://www.thefreesite.com is a good place to go for free stuff. You will find animated images, seamless backgrounds, java scripts, counters, horizontal bars, free graphic and font programs... and if you don't find it here, there are scores of links to other useful sites. Most of the information is easy to access and to integrate into your web pages.

COVER DISKS

Another source of inspiration and free tools are computer magazines' cover disks. They often feature free clip arts and free fonts for your PC. Check out the computer section at your local newsagent from time to time.

INDEX